GO DO DEALS

GO DO DEALS

THE ENTREPRENEUR'S GUIDE TO BUYING & SELLING BUSINESSES

JEREMY HARBOUR

NEW YORK

LONDON • NASHVILLE • MELBOURNE • VANCOUVER

GO DO DEALS
THE ENTREPRENEUR'S GUIDE
TO BUYING & SELLING BUSINESSES

© 2021 **JEREMY HARBOUR**

Published in New York, New York, by Morgan James Publishing. Morgan James is a trademark of Morgan James, LLC. www.MorganJamesPublishing.com

ISBN 978-1-63195-293-7 paperback
ISBN 978-1-63195-294-4 eBook
ISBN 978-1-63195-292-0 hardcover
Library of Congress Control Number: 2020915459

Morgan James is a proud partner of Habitat for Humanity Peninsula and Greater Williamsburg. Partners in building since 2006.

Get involved today! Visit
www.MorganJamesBuilds.com

DISCLAIMER

Don't blame me. I made it all up. Don't do anything I say, unless it's a raging success—in which case it was definitely all me.

For Simona, Ariella, and Aiden

CONTENTS

FOREWORD
DOING DEALS CHANGES YOUR LIFE

There's that moment where something big is agreed, and your future shifts as a result. Most people will only ever do just a few life-changing deals—entering their marriage, starting a business, and buying a home being among the bigger ones.

A small number of people do a lot of deals. They buy and sell many properties, start several businesses, acquire their competitors, find investors to back their ideas, secure the rights to intellectual property, get publishing contracts to write a book, or any number of life-changing deals that are there to be done.

Most people have not recognized that living a big, exciting life is linked to the ability to do deals.

Without this realization, they aren't even looking for life-changing deals, and, subsequently, they walk past ten of them a month.

In many ways, this was me before I met Jeremy Harbour. I had started and grown a successful business, but I was focused only on one type of deal-making sales. As a small business owner, my mind was focused on the day-to-day operations of my business, and, naturally, a big part of that was finding customers. I had trained my mind to always be on the lookout for potential clients, and I didn't see much else.

When I started spending time with Jeremy, things changed. He radically challenged my thinking about business and life. He seemed to be playing by a different set of rules, and his rules were producing remarkable results.

I met Jeremy at an entrepreneurs' networking event and discovered that he had thirteen businesses but didn't run any of them day-to-day. He employed people he had never met; he made money from products that he had never personally sold. What's more, he hadn't started any of these businesses; he had bought them—he'd done deals to acquire them.

Over the years, I witnessed Jeremy buying and selling businesses very quickly and often with very little of his own money in the deal. He bought a variety of businesses—a gym, a technology provider, a fashion retailer, a training company, a commercial kitchen cleaning business, an air-conditioning repair company—and every time we talked, he had another deal on the go.

He then sold these businesses for vast gains. Often, he would structure a deal that would see him earning money from a deal for the following three to five years.

What impressed me most was that, when I met people Jeremy was doing deals with, they all spoke highly of him. He created win-win deals, expanding the horizons for all parties involved. To this day, I've not met a person who wouldn't do more deals with Jeremy.

When the global financial crisis threatened to melt down economies around the world, most people were scared and gloomy. I was shocked to see how excited Jeremy was at the prospect of so many deals that were now available to be done. He snapped up dozens of deals during that time and made extraordinary sums of money along the way.

Fortunately, I started to catch on to this new approach. Jeremy's words echoed in my mind: "If you do more deals, you'll live a bigger, better life."

I went out and did several deals that changed things for me, too. I raised investment to grow my business, I did four acquisitions, and took a stake in half a dozen companies. I exited a deal and bought out a business partner. Jeremy was right; doing deals changed things rapidly.

While I was getting better at doing small business deals, Jeremy shifted his focus onto bigger deals. He began looking into the world of private equity and public markets. He researched intensely for over a year before creating a deal structure now known as an "Agglomeration." This deal structure saw him launch a "collaborative IPO" on the Nasdaq, where over twenty businesses went from being private companies to publicly-traded stock.

Doing big deals has led to a big life for Jeremy. His typical year consists of travelling to his houses around the world, spending time on his luxury boats (two of them), and going on dream holidays every few months. Not bad for a guy who dropped out of high school and started his career trading trinkets at weekend market stalls.

The book you have in your hands is a generous gift. It covers key ideas and core principles Jeremy has deployed to build up his empire. For the cost of a pub meal, you'll start to see how you could buy the pub with little or none of your own money.

After reading this book, you'll look at the world differently and recognize how many hundreds of potential deals you've already walked right past without knowing it. If ever there's another financial crisis or recession, you'll probably get excited rather than scared at the prospect of so many opportunities to do deals.

You'll also see many of your business role models differently. You'll recognize that Richard Branson has been doing deals a lot more than businesses. You'll see that the meteoric rise of Google is just as much a story of acquisitions and deal flow as it is a story of technology and innovation. You'll look at Bill Gates differently: he built Microsoft on a series of big deals. Even creatives like JK Rowling or Oprah have made their fortunes through deals.

The ideas in this book will challenge your thinking, give you new strategies, and change the way you do business. Hopefully, as a result of this book, you will go and do deals that completely change your life for the better.

—Daniel Priestley
Entrepreneur and Best-Selling Author

PREFACE
THE STORY OF THE HARBOUR CLUB

I have always been business-sector agnostic, and so my first deals were in a wide range of industries including telecom, IT, a health club and spa, and a music school. After I had done a dozen or so of my own deals, I started to get a bit of a reputation for doing deals without using any of my own money or borrowing from banks.

I had people chasing me to work for them in some capacity, either as a non-executive director or on some sort of consultancy basis, to help them acquire companies for no money down. I just couldn't think of any good reason why on earth I would want to do that. When I find a company that I can buy for $1, I just buy it. Why would I want a salary to do that for someone else?

Then one day, I bought a business seminar company. It made me think that perhaps an educational program could be a way to work with these aspiring dealmakers to give them the tools and tactics needed to acquire companies themselves. This would create potential future partners who understood my methodology, and they would have no qualms about making deals on their own because they would have paid for the information.

So, as I was sitting in one of the seminars from my recently acquired business, the Harbour Club was born. Then, something fascinating happened. Before this time, I'd been like a butterfly going from flower to flower—or in my case, from deal to deal. I had never stopped to analyze the process I went through when considering a deal. The first thing did was to go through each of my previous deals and explored what worked, what didn't work, and what could be effectively repeated. I found quite a few things I had done that had worked, but I had never done again!

So, by precisely analyzing what it was I had been doing, I created a framework of processes and systems. I did my first-ever Harbour Club course in 2009—an intensive, all-inclusive, three-day seminar. We've done a few courses every year since and every time, there are more real deals completed, more important lessons learned, and more valuable ideas shared.

The course has grown in both size and content over the years from the lessons and tactics I have honed while personally completing dozens of deals and from feedback on the hundreds of deals done by Harbour Club delegates. Attendees receive completely out-of-the-box approaches to doing no-money-down deals that simply are not available anywhere else. Through sheer volume, we are evolving and developing our tactics all the time, constantly improving, and adding new angles and structures that have been properly field-tested. There is no other mergers and acquisitions (M & A) course that comes close to being able to offer such a suite of tools and solutions to its participants. Also, belonging to a global network of members with a wide range of skills is invaluable in getting more deals done and extending learning. Our closed social network holds regular meetups, chat groups, and video conferences to share our experiences.

But I don't make my money selling training. I make my money doing deals. I am a deal junkie first and foremost, and the Harbour Club is my network of dealmakers. As such, if you become involved with the Harbour Club, you will not be subjected to high-pressure sales of products or courses. We simply run our events at full price for the first visit and offer a massive discount for you to return to gain new information and meet new people the next time.

All the mastermind groups, chats, ongoing advice, and help within the delegate network are free. Our best dealmakers take natural leadership positions, sharing their stories and experiences, and helping people to get deals done. In every Harbour Club group course, there are now deep dive case studies into recent deals done by recent graduates. You hear not just about my experiences, but also about those who have completed the course and implemented the tactics. They share what they have learned by putting the tactics to use.

It is often thought that we just buy distressed bankrupt businesses that are about to close down. This could not be further from the truth. There are (at the time of writing) twelve no-money-down deal structures that we teach. Only two of these are for buying "just about to die" businesses, and both show you how to do it in a low-risk and high-reward way. The rest of these structures enable you to buy good, and even great, businesses. We have case studies of people buying profitable, debt-free businesses with seven figures of assets on the balance sheet, no cash up front, and no debt. We have had members buy long-established, well-known companies with businesses with revenues of up to $12 million. It is all about understanding people's motivations and creating the right deal structure to meet their needs.

INTRODUCTION

In 2012, I wrote an Amazon bestselling book titled Go Do. It was a summary of my life in business to that date and a compassionate butt-kicking to everyone who talks about starting a business but never quite gets around to it. To this day, I am humbled by the stories and messages I receive from those who have read the book and been affected by it in some way.

There are loads of books on starting up a business, sales and marketing, systematization, management, leadership, and every variation of working harder or smarter, but there's not much in the way of, "and now what?" books. You have a business. You have sales. You have a brand. Now what? I find it frustrating that, while there has been a boom in social science-type titles in the last decade or so, there simply hasn't been anything new in the business strategy book space.

To understand the next steps, you have to understand what the key drivers are for being an entrepreneur in the first place. Most people would say freedom, whether that is the freedom to pursue a passion, freedom to develop a product, or freedom of your time or finances. What invariably happens for most entrepreneurs is that, in your pursuit of freedom, you unwittingly build a new prison. It's one you can't take a vacation from, occupies your every waking thought, challenges your relationships, steals your time, pillages your finances, and at various stages, teaches you all thirty-eight flavors of stress and heartache. Now don't get me wrong: all these things are hugely valuable human experiences. I wouldn't trade them for anything, but there has to be a point where the masochism stops, and you get some clear air. That's when the next steps are the most valuable.

I believe the next step, that next rung of the ladder, is adding deal-making to your entrepreneurial repertoire. Buying and selling companies is a core component of taking the entrepreneurial experience to the next level.

If you look at any successful entrepreneur, you will see that they grew by acquisition or created wealth through an exit of some sort, whether a sale (like Elon Musk or Richard Branson) or an initial public offering (an IPO, like Bill Gates or Mark Zuckerberg). I believe that an acquisition is the only way a business can double its size "in an afternoon" and sometimes the only way it can grow or break through to the next level. Have you noticed that there seems to be a glass ceiling on company size in many industries, where you find thousands of similar-sized competitors and a few larger players? Well, a solid plan to become one of the larger players is to mop up a number of smaller companies to give you a quick scale.

You can break the scale paradox (this is how I describe the phenomenon that 'you have to be big to get big') by punching above your weight with suppliers and winning larger contracts to create even more revenue and profit so that the constraints that kept you small are quickly shrugged off.

The Entrepreneur's Contribution

You are basically selling your future income Small business owners have to level up. According to the Organisation for Economic Co-operation and Development (OECD), small- and medium-sized enterprises (SMEs) represent 50% of gross domestic product (GDP) and 98% of private-sector employment in most major economies. This is an extraordinary contribution, yet the wealthy owners are few and far between. They are the exceptions, not the rule. I have dedicated myself to helping reconnect value creation to wealth, to make it not only cool to be an entrepreneur, but financially rewarding—in effect, to create a meritocratic way to democratize wealth (a way that entrepreneurs can be rewarded based on the merits of the value they've created).

I believe that, if entrepreneurs added a "growth-by-acquisition engine" to their existing organic growth strategy, they would quickly improve their businesses and create a good deal of shareholder value. It is only by creating more shareholder value that we can achieve the freedoms we foresaw when we started.

A common misconception is that vast amounts of capital are needed to grow by acquisition. This is simply not true. I have done dozens of deals with no capital, and my delegates in the Harbour Club have done hundreds more. Often it is more about meeting the seller's needs and more about the deal structure than the price. For example, distressed deals can be a great way to add new customers and revenue with no cash up front.

My first-ever deal was with someone you might call a "motivated" seller. In a single transaction, I added a year's worth of sales to my business. I call these "tactical acquisitions"—simple deals that grow your business quickly. Large companies, like Facebook, do dozens of these kinds of deals every month.

But the companies in question don't have to be distressed; you can do deals with perfectly solvent, profitable, debt-free companies that are well run. How? By focusing on the needs of the owners and working out a structure that is a win-win but doesn't involve lots of cash up front.

You also don't need debt. Many people use working capital finance to do deals, and this can get toxic, fast, and giving that money to a key employee…to leave!

Would You Ask a Barber If You Needed a Haircut?

Unfortunately, solid information about how to buy and sell companies is limited. The available books tend to be written by Master of Business Administration (MBA) professors, advisers, lawyers, accountants, corporate finance people, or business brokers—enterprises that make money by helping people buy or sell companies.

The books written by advisers and brokers are inherently flawed. Advisers always say, "Surround yourself with advisers." Of course they're going to say that. You can spend a fortune on advisers. Most of the corporate finance companies and legal firms will require a down payment or monthly retainers to engage them, sometimes running to tens of thousands of dollars. People who are taking fees on an ongoing basis until you've done a deal are actually incentivized not to do the deal. At best, they're incentivized to drag it out for as long as possible.

Business brokers can be on the buy-side or the sell-side of a transaction. They're traditionally incentivized because they receive a percentage of what you pay for the business. There's not much impetus for them to try and support a 'no-money-down' transaction—where's the money in that deal for them? If there is no cash day one, there is nothing to pay them from. They might suggest the leveraged buy-out (LBO) model, which is, of course, one way to buy a business. There's no shortage of information on how to do an LBO. On Amazon, there are currently over 280 books on the topic of how to buy a business with no money down by using lots of debt.

Deals are done by two people. Ultimately, it's a face-to-face thing. It's about trust and rapport, and the more people you involve in that discussion, the less likely it is that the deal will happen. The deal team that the brokers advise you to use creates a problem as they often interfere in the relationship that you're trying to create.

You can't build a marriage with a bunch of other people involved, continually giving you advice on what you should say and do, and how you should approach specific conversations. It doesn't work like that.

Brokers and advisers subordinate the best advice by saying, "Get the best lawyer, or the best accountant, or the best corporate finance company you can afford." Rather than standing by their advice, they just tell you to pay for more advisors. It is a lazy technique that does not reflect how the real world works (or can work), and it's not particularly helpful if you're running a small to mid-size enterprise (SME) and you want to acquire one of your competitors. You could easily spend more on legal fees than you spend on acquiring the company.

One of the delegates who gave an in-depth case study at a recent Harbour Club course made a great remark. "I took the owner of the business for a coffee, and by the end of it, the coffee cost more than the company."

Get Smart, Then Go Do Deals

It is a question of being armed with the right tools to go and do the deals. In this book, I'm going to give you some of the many tools, sub-tools, and tactics that you will need to accomplish this. We evolve our advice constantly, as hundreds of Harbour Club members around the world do deals every day. Their experience flows back into the group through the Harbour Club online forums and the various groups that get together regularly, either face to face, Zoom, or discussions in the Harbour Club app.

xxiv | **GO DO DEALS**

I called this book *Go Do Deals* partly in homage to my first book, *Go Do,* but mainly because that is the only way you are going to learn how to create your own deal-making success. As with learning a new language, you learn best by immersion. You have to start by immersing yourself in deals and learn by doing. From doing comes confidence and a track record. Then more deals come along, and soon there's an avalanche of deals waiting to be done.

It can be a little scary to leap into the unknown, to do a deal and just see what happens, but I hope that with the knowledge from this book and the understanding of the risks and how to mitigate them, you'll gain enough confidence to dive in.

Then . . . Go do deals!

PART ONE

WHY YOU SHOULD GO DO DEALS

Sometimes you win. Sometimes you learn.

A Note on Rewarding Value Creation

The world is not fair. Inequality is a global issue. Its presence is hard not to notice, as it is in every political speech, on TV, in films, and especially when you travel. Yet global living standards have risen exponentially. Don't believe the media: levels of absolute poverty have been coming down year by year, and globalization has much to do with the elevation of living standards.

The real issue isn't poverty or living standards: inequality is about the perceived unevenness of the distribution of wealth, with the super-wealthy getting wealthier. It is relative poverty that drives the politics of envy.

Real equality is about equality of opportunity, and we have made leaps forward in this regard. Over the last thirty years, there has been a massive change in wealth and—more importantly—in wealth distribution. When I was growing up, the richest person in the world was the Sultan of Brunei, and the Queen of England was one of the twenty wealthiest people in the UK. Today, there is only one hereditary billionaire in the *Sunday Times* Rich List top ten, and the majority of billionaires and multimillionaires are self-made in one generation. This is unprecedented.

But this is still only 1% of the 1%, and there is a very long tail on the graph after that. All governments and political commentators talk about the problem of inequality. The recent populist movements are driven by a frustration, felt globally, that there seems to be a glass ceiling for most and unlimited riches for others. This frustration gets directed at rich people, immigrants, governments, secret societies, or anyone else people can think of. All governments can seem to come up with is variations on the idea of taking money from people who work hard and take risks in order to give it to those who don't. It has been demonstrated again and again throughout history that this model is not sustainable. There has to be a better answer.

For entrepreneurs, it is like a bet you can only lose. If you fail, you lose everything; if you win, you lose most of it. Entrepreneurs are society's change agents.

Nearly every life-changing breakthrough or innovation has been born of the mind of an entrepreneur or has been commercialized by an entrepreneur who has made it work. These people bet everything—their relationships, their health, their money—because they want to change something. When they see an itch that needs to be scratched, they scratch it. When they see a problem that can be solved, they solve it. When they solve these problems, they get paid. That is value, and that value is created by entrepreneurs every day.

Ultimately though, these problem solvers are not rewarded. Global capital has become detached from value creation. In any mature economy, SMEs represent around 50% of GDP and 95–99% of private-sector employment (depending on where they are located). SMEs are vital to the economy, job creation, tax contribution, and the health of the economy.

I believe we can take control of wealth and investment, and that we can eliminate the bank's intermediary role in controlling the money supply and the government's role in wealth redistribution. We can also get thousands of new wealthy entrepreneurs solving the world's biggest problems instead of fighting every day against a system that is completely skewed against them.

As an entrepreneur, it's your duty to do deals. In this section, we're going to look at why you won't make money running your business, why it's OK to be a novice, and how you should position yourself as an investor.

Everything we need to do this is already out there. We just need to get on and do it. We can be caring, compassionate, and capitalists. They are not mutually exclusive.

Now, go forth and do deals!

CHAPTER 1

YOU DON'T MAKE MONEY RUNNING BUSINESSES

Running a business is for schmucks.

Entrepreneurs often fall into the trap of thinking that you have to work hard at running your business to get wealthy. I'm going to show you that this is not necessarily the case. It's still hard work, but your hard work should be invested elsewhere, so that you can see truly spectacular results in short periods of time.

You might think you have read all the books on buying and selling businesses; however, rather than focusing on practical tips and entrepreneurial ways to acquire and sell businesses, they focus on the need for expert accountants and lawyers to broker the deals. At the Harbour Club, I share with my delegates practical tips and advice from my personal experience using relevant examples, which have been implemented and proven for more than twenty years.

Look at Richard Branson: at the early stage of his career, he executed a huge deal that was his game-changer. He made his money when he *sold* Virgin Music to Thorn EMI for roughly $960 million. Before that day, he admits he was borderline insolvent. Another example is Brian Acton, co-founder of WhatsApp. Brian made his money when he and co-founder, Jan Koum, sold WhatsApp to Facebook in 2014 for $19 billion.

Both of these well-known entrepreneurs only became wealthy when they sold their own business or acquired and sold another business. Businessmen and women who have secured real wealth are usually less operationally involved in their businesses, leaving them more time to think strategically about the bigger picture.

Deal Deep Dive: The Telecom Company

In 1997, I started a telecommunications company. After running the business for a few years, I started to notice that, every week, I was being approached by other telecom companies who wanted to buy my business. Interestingly, they all had one thing in common: they had no money—well, none that they were willing to give *me*. What they did offer were deal structures with what I call "jam tomorrow"(an empty, useless promise of something that will never arrive or be fulfilled) and a solution to some of the pain and problems of running a business, like ironing out cash flow, dealing with staff, finding customers, providing capital to grow, and locating flashy office space.

The telecom industry is especially acquisitive because everything is duplicated in telecom companies. When you combine two telecom companies, there are now two offices, two finance directors, two billing systems, and two IT systems. A two-plus-two deal can equal ten after you take away all of the cost base from one company. For this reason, most telecom companies have a mergers and acquisitions (M&A) strategy in place alongside their organic growth strategy.

So why wasn't I thinking like this? After all, I too didn't have any money! Maybe I should be the buyer and not the seller? Why was I still asking people the more operational questions like, "How many mobile phones do you have?" I wasn't thinking strategically. I wasn't acting like an entrepreneur. I was basically a glorified salesperson. In the end, I met with many potential buyers but couldn't decide on any deal. It was like being at a restaurant with a huge selection of meals on the menu; it's impossible to choose, and you end up not ordering anything. My thinking went full circle, and I thought, "I'm going to be the buyer." So began my journey to acquire another business.

Now I had this new idea in my head—I'm going to buy a business! I needed to have conversations with people about buying businesses. I needed to have strategic conversations, and I needed to get in front of a lot of people, so I went networking.

At one networking event, I came across another telecom company based in Slough in the UK. They'd been going for thirteen years, had some really good customers and supplied lots of companies on the Slough trading estate. One of their customers was Nintendo. I was pretty young and unconvincing at the time, so it was lucky for me that the owner had a perfect storm of motivations for selling. His three urgent and pressing needs helped me to break my deal virginity and get that first deal done.

The owner's three motivations to sell were as follows:

1. **The ticking time bomb:** He operated from a retail outlet close to the Slough trading estate (the largest business park in Europe with over 500 businesses and 20,000 employees) and most of his customers were businesses in the area that appreciated the

proximity. We were based close by, but we operated from an office, delivering phones to our customers or having customers pick them up them from us. We didn't need to be a retail establishment, and we weren't wedded to the idea of operating from retail premises. The lease on his shop was about to expire, and the landlord had decided to bulldoze the building and turn it into apartments. He had a ticking time bomb—he needed to be out of the premises within a specific time frame and was furiously looking for a new space.

Finding a retail outlet in this area was difficult because of the expense. The owner of the telecom company needed a rent deposit up front, fit-out costs, and, of course, the relocation expenses. He'd estimated it was going to cost him around $70,000 to move. The business in the previous year had made a net profit of $12,000, so the next few years' profits were going to be eaten up by the forced move. He wasn't relishing running the business for another five years of his life just to stand still.

2. **Frustration of changing goalposts:** At the time, there were only two Internet service providers, Cellnet and Vodafone. Vodafone had a specific third- party channel approach to its business, using dealerships and intermediaries. They looked after their dealer base. Cellnet kept changing focus: at one point it would be very third-party channel-focused, then it would go through a direct channel focus, then it would move back to a third-party focus. The telecom business was with Cellnet, and the rules and operating procedures changed regularly. The owner would quote a customer for a particular product or service, and a couple of months later, when the customer said yes he could no longer deliver it at the price they had agreed. This created unmitigated frustration.

Business Breakout: Vodafone

Vodafone went on to become, at one point, the largest mobile phone company on the planet, while Cellnet always struggled, eventually having to rebrand. It was bought and sold a couple of times. The path that Vodafone adopted was definitely more successful and their model was very acquisitive. They would create third-party relationships; the unhealthy companies would go bust and Vodafone would buy the good ones. They used deals and acquisitions as a way of integrating vertically with their supply chain without taking all the risk. The marketing and investment in systems that the service providers had to do did not appear on Vodafone's balance sheet, but, if they worked, they became part of Vodafone's success.

3. **Shiny object syndrome:** This is something all entrepreneurs suffer from, in that their favorite business is always the next one. They want to rush out and deploy the idea they just thought about in the shower. And when they start that side hustle, that extra business, they end up loving it more than the old one. Their thinking is: "I've been running this business for thirteen years, it takes up all my time, it's stressful, it's hard work, but this new thing could be worth a gazillion dollars in the next five minutes if I just had the resources and the time to focus on it."

In this particular case, the owner of the telecom business was buying two-story row homes in the area near his shop and converting them into duplex apartments. Whenever he did one of these conversions, he made about $70,000 profit. He was doing a couple a year, but he would have been able to do around six a year—and massively improve his income—if he had more time and wasn't sitting in the shop all day waiting for customers. He loved doing those property conversions. It was that passion that got him up in the morning. Becoming free to pursue this passion was a powerful motivation.

Those three motivations—the ticking time bomb of lease expiration, his service provider driving him insane, and the fact that he could make more money if he wasn't running the telecom business—were enough to drive him to do the deal.

So, we had a deal, but my next challenge was that I didn't know how to buy a company. At the networking and breakfast meetings, I would zone in on the accountants and lawyers and quiz them about buying a company. I would pepper them with questions: What actually has to happen? How do you transfer the shares? What forms do you fill out? What legal contracts do you need?

Business Breakout: Buy the Company

The overriding principle, all the lawyers told me (and I must have spoken to a dozen), was, "Don't buy the company. Buy the assets of the company because there could be skeletons in the closet." (We explore this topic fully in the Harbour Club because now I don't believe that's the right way to do it. In most of the deals I do, I do buy the company—particularly one in a distressed situation—because you can then control any bankruptcy process and, if there are skeletons in the closet, you can work to get rid of the skeletons. If you're not in control of that process, then it can cause much trouble further down the line.)

Back then, I was told to just buy the assets, so that's what I was going to do.

An asset purchase agreement was a bit like using a sledgehammer to crack a nut, based on the size of this particular deal. So, after various discussions, we decided that the easiest way would be to write a letter of agreement that we would both sign, specifying what assets were being sold, for what price, and on what terms.

We sat down and drafted the letter. He wanted £15,000 up front for all the customers, stock, and goodwill—basically the assets of the business. If I'd had £15,000 in my bank, I'd have written a check there and then. The deal was worth a huge amount to me because right away, just by switching their customers over, I could get a windfall of six figures. I would get sign-on commissions for every contract I migrated from Cellnet to Vodafone, so it was an absolute no-brainer for me, but the problem was I didn't have the money.

I had absolutely no money when I started this telecom company. I had £50 that I spent on business cards. The money from my first sale went to buy a computer. It was truly that kind of hand-to-mouth business from the beginning. But we were growing pretty fast.

Business Breakout: The Agreement

A handshake or a verbal agreement is legally binding. The only reason we write it down is so that we have evidence as to what was agreed. The idea that you have to use a lawyer and that the agreement has to be thirty pages is nonsense, particularly when it comes to the distressed opportunity type of deals. Besides which, the other side probably can't afford a lawyer, so if you have one, they'll feel that it's unfair. Most lawyers will only deal with other lawyers because they want to be sure that the other parties involved have proper legal advice.

Now, most interpretation of the law is about intent. As long as you can make the intention clearly known, you can be reasonably covered in anything that might arise from a dispute. If you have to speak in front of a judge, the judge will read whatever documents you signed to try to understand what the intent was at the time that you signed them, and then pass a judgment. On that basis, to get the intent clear is easy—you just write it in plain English, collaboratively, with each party contributing to the wording.

It always surprises me when I get legal agreements written in anything but plain English. You know, the type where they spend the first few pages defining words they might use, and then add loads of ambiguous paragraphs that seem to loop back and contradict each other. If I were being cynical, I would say that they're potentially creating work for themselves in the future, when the contract has to be tested and they're the only ones who understand how it was put together in the first place. If you can write something clearly which everyone can understand, that's legally binding.

Business Breakout: Beware of Telecoms

I chose telecom even though it is a capital-intensive industry. There were dozens of other businesses I could have chosen that would scale up without the need for so much investment. As a telecom company, with every customer you sign up, you lose money! You make that money back over the contract term of the customer. The more you sell, the less money you have. It was probably not the smartest business for me to go into at that time, but I had made my bed and now I had to lie in it.

My choice that month was, do I pay my credit card bill, or do I pay my staff? The idea of paying £15,000 for an acquisition wasn't even in the cards. It couldn't work. So, I came up with various proposals for how we could pay the owner of the telecom company on acquiring customers, or on a deferred basis, or over a period of time. He then said he wanted £10,000 up front and a little bit later). Then, alternatively, £5,000 up front and the rest later.

In my naivety, I hadn't realized that I was the only horse in the race. This guy had just a few weeks left on his lease. He was never going to find somebody who would be able to complete the due diligence and come up with the cash in such a short space of time. But in my head, I was convinced that he had loads of other potential opportunities and that if I didn't strike quickly, I was going to lose out on an amazing deal. I bought into his paradigm a little too much. I should probably have just said, "Here's the deal. Take it or leave it.

Instead, I continued to nedogiate and try to find the money. I called friends, customers, and everybody I could think of to try and raise the cash to be able to give him something. I got down to £2,500 up front, and I couldn't even lay my hands on that. The only deal that could happen was zero up front. The day the bulldozers were due to arrive was the day we closed the deal.

After I acquired that business, I had the most incredible feeling— like I had found a door into another dimension and walked in. I'd been so wedded to the idea that you start a business, you work really hard, and success comes from all this hard work. Yet, I had grown by a year's worth of sales in an afternoon without any sales, marketing, risk, or cash outlay.

Necessity is the mother of invention. Quite often, when I give a speech to a business group, I'm asked, "Well, how do you buy a business without any money," and my facetious answer is, "It's really easy. First, you start with no money, then go and try and buy a business." Because that was the essence of it for me: the only option available to me was to complete a transaction without any cash up front.

I learned that you don't have to run a marathon to grow your business; you can just run the last ten yards and you still get the medal. By acquiring a business as a growth strategy, it's possible to grow by a year's worth of sales or more in an afternoon. This forced me to think more strategically, more like an investor or shareholder. It was an epiphany. I had just dismantled everything I believed to be true: I had found a hack for value creation that didn't involve blood, sweat, and years.

CHAPTER 2

TO BECOME AN EXPERT,
YOU MUST START AS A NOVICE

Experience is what you get
when you don't get what you want.

I did my first deal over twenty years ago. I knew absolutely nothing about doing deals at that point. Despite all of my experience, I often say I understand 10% of my chosen field, which doesn't sound like much, but that is 9% more than nearly everyone else.

It's a hugely complex area, and I don't expect anyone to become an expert by taking one training course or reading one book or going to one seminar. There is no substitute for learning other than by doing, but what you can do is to arm yourself with the tools and tactics to avoid the common mistakes.

When I'm teaching at the Harbour Club, I always talk about the importance of breaking your deal virginity, getting that first deal done, and how valuable that experience is. It becomes a proof of concept for you. It is almost a mental reset. It clears away the doubt and gives you a confidence visible to the people you are doing deals with. That is infectious and simply leads to more deals.

You might be finding it difficult to comprehend or validate the fact that you can even do a deal. People often try to rationalize it by saying, for example, "If I built a $5 million-a-year business, I wouldn't give it up," and this holds them back. (This is a false belief, and sometimes people look through their own lens and misunderstand.) Once you've done one deal, you then know that it's possible. That's a hugely powerful realization. This is almost the opposite of what I experienced with my first deal: a feeling of doing something a part of me was telling me couldn't be done. After all, according to the laws of physics, the bumblebee can't fly, but nobody's told the bumblebee yet.

Having no money was the best thing that could have happened to me at that time, because if I'd had the money, I would have paid the owner of the telecom company. I would have continued to live in the belief that you always have to pay some cash up front in every deal. This is a paradigm that many people are stuck in. Most people who come to the Harbour Club course are stuck here.

Sometimes, even after they've done the Harbour Club course, I catch them trying to pay money up front for a deal. It's interesting how quickly you forget these lessons and default to conventional wisdom, despite the overwhelming evidence to the contrary. I did my next few deals without using any cash up front, and then, because I'd started to make some money (by doing deals instead of just running a business), I accidentally started paying for deals.

There were four or five deals in a row where I had to put a little cash on the table up front. It was only when I caught myself doing it that I decided to make this like a sport—a game where the object is not to spend a penny.

So, I doubled my determination and decided to make sure that none of my deals would involve any cash up front. Ever. Even when confronted with the most obvious of no-brainer bargains, I would still stick to my no-cash guns. This sometimes amused my colleagues, who simply couldn't understand why I was so adamant about no cash up front. These were mostly distressed deals with motivated sellers, so often, they didn't have many other opportunities. This took me time to realize, though, and I would often fall for their confidence, believing that buyers were lined up, and get what I call "deal heat"—a desire to get the deal done regardless. Today, I am confident that I am probably the only game in town, even if the sellers are talking to dozens of other people. I know that the others will get bogged down in due diligence, and I can run off with the business before they even have an engagement letter from their lawyer.

The Hospital Pass

Most of the time, these distressed business owners were considering closing the doors and walking away. In these deals, they were giving me a "hospital pass." This is a rugby expression whereby you're only allowed to tackle somebody if they're holding the ball, so if you've got some big guy running toward you, you pass the ball to someone else, and they get clobbered (straight to the hospital). Giving a hospital pass in business happens when people feel they have exhausted all avenues and now have to do what is undoubtedly the worst part of being an entrepreneur: laying everyone off, failing to make payroll, and basically locking the doors and walking away from years of their life's work.

What I learned from running a horrendously undercapitalized telecom company was how to be incredibly efficient with cash, and how to manage a cash-based company on a shoestring budget. Often, when the owners thought they were completely bankrupt, these hospital pass businesses were unaware of opportunities and things that they could do slightly differently to save their businesses. We could rescue them.

Because I didn't have the money to start a telecom company, it meant I learned how to run a lean ship. The fact that I didn't have any money meant that I learned how to do deals without any money. You don't become an expert by watching, you learn by doing. So, what should you be doing?

Move Up the Entrepreneur's Ladder

You need to stop dealing (read: "interfering") with staff and customers and start to focus on the strategic areas of the company. These are:

Mergers: A merger is simply an acquisition using shares as the consideration (payment). It's particularly helpful to create scale and solve succession planning (more on that in a later chapter). In practical terms, you normally create a new holding company, and the shareholders in the two merging entities share in this new entity. Both companies remain intact but, instead of you owning one company 100%, you own a percentage of a holding company with two (or more) subsidiaries. This holding company reports its financial results consolidated as the sum of the parts: you add up the two sets of accounts, so that 2 × $1 million revenue companies = 1 × $2 million revenue company.

Acquisitions: This is the only way I know to double the size of your business tomorrow. Every business should have an acquisition strategy along with its organic growth strategy and should devote as much time and attention to it as well. These deals will create the big steps up in the business, the multi-year shortcuts, and opportunities for new products, markets, and fresh talent.

Joint Ventures: Partnerships can massively scale your business and play to your strengths while leveraging others' strengths. They can also create credibility and brand extension.

Exit: When you are looking for capital events that will transform your wealth and your life, your best customer is the one who buys your business. We need to ditch the idea that your entire career culminates in one "end of life" deal. You should have regular capital events. You don't make money-running businesses. You make money when you sell. So sell—often! This significantly lowers your risk and provides a much better lifestyle and more security, leading to better decision-making.

Ask yourself, what do you do every day? If the answer is mergers, acquisitions, joint ventures, or exits, you've moved up the ladder. If you're still interfering in the day-to-day business, you need to learn by doing deals. Get that first deal under your belt.

Somebody always has to be the first customer or the first deal, but the second deal can be easier because you have the experience, plus the reference point of the first customer. Through the Harbour Club, we help you create partnerships and joint ventures with people who have gone through it before, so they can help you break your deal virginity. I did it without that community. I did it without having those people around me, so it's possible for everybody.

Deals are done in rapport, by making friends with the person you're doing a deal with, or at least creating trust and respect and an environment where a deal can happen. A huge part of building trust and empathy comes from the fact that you've done it before, or you have some shared experiences and pains. If you've got even a tiny deal under your belt, you can talk about it. Even if it was a disaster, you have a reference point for future conversations.

While I can give you tools, tactics, and information, nothing is going to help like getting out there and getting the first deal under your belt. You have to do the first deal before you can get the second one.

Deal Deep Dive: IT Company on a Plate

Back at my telecom company, we had a managing director, an operations director, and a financial controller. After doing my first deal with the small telecom company, I sat down with my little board of directors, full of the joys of spring, excited that we could scale really quickly, picking businesses up for no money down. I'd done one deal, so I was sure I could find loads more if I just got out there. Then I said the fateful words: "In fact, it doesn't even have to be a telecom company. We could just buy anything."

At this point, one of the directors shouted:

"Whoa, whoa, Jeremy, calm down, come back to reality. We really need to focus on growing telecom. Yes, this is a great little deal, and if we could do one of those every six to nine months, it would be a fantastic second engine on our plane so that we have the organic growth engine and this new acquisitive growth engine. That would be fantastic, but let's not buy a pub. Let's stick to what we know and buy telcos."

I defended my position; I really wanted to buy whatever came along. If I saw a business I could buy for a buck, why wouldn't I just buy it? Wouldn't it be incredibly frustrating not to do a deal just because it wasn't in the telco sector? We could buy it and we could sell it, or we could buy it and we could use it as a service provider or whatever. After a long debate, we finally agreed that we could also buy an IT company. Telecom and IT were converging at this time, so there were crossover products like Voice over Internet Protocol (VoIP) and BlackBerry, products that were as much computer as they were telecom. IT and telecoms were definitely on a convergent path.

A few weeks later, while we were doing job interviews for an account manager (I wasn't allowed to do interviews on my own because I just talk at applicants relentlessly for a couple of hours and then offer them the job), one interviewee passed his CV across, showing that the last job he'd had was in an IT business that had his family name. I saw an opportunity and started to quiz him. He was running a small IT company from home, just himself and two engineers, doing network support and network installation. They'd been in business a few years, so why was he looking for a job? He explained:

> "Well, the problem is it's quite a small business, so I always pay the engineers first. Then I pay myself when cash flow allows. Sometimes that's the end of the month, and sometimes it's a week later. Because of the network support nature, we often end up working funny hours like weekends and evenings. My wife is pregnant, so the room in the house that I call the office she calls the nursery.
>
> The hours and the pay situation are making her worried. When she has the baby, she would quite like some support, and to know that she can buy diapers."

The Deal Sitting in the Room

I was thinking, "Wow, these things just fall into our lap. Three weeks ago, we said we wanted an IT company, and lo and behold, here is an IT company." When the interviewee left the room, I turned to my operations director, "Can you believe that? Isn't that amazing?" And my operations director said, "Yeah, he would make a great account manager."

I was blown away that he didn't see the deal sitting in the room with us even though he was in the same meeting. It was then that I realized that the human brain has amazing filtering capabilities. We're bombarded with billions and billions of things on a daily basis, and we filter everything that doesn't fit within our frame of interest. My frame of interest, like a dog with a bone, was doing that next deal. How am I going to get another deal? I was absolutely tuned in to DEAL-FM and the desire to do the next transaction. What amazed me was that other people weren't.

We bought his business for $1, ironed out his lumpy cash-flow problems, and gave him a job in our company with regular wages, working hours, and security.

———————

Many people come to the Harbour Club in the same situation. There are signposts popping up and opportunities available every day, and they're just not seeing them. They're not wearing the spectacles through which they see deals everywhere, so they're missing opportunities. We talk more about this in Chapter 4.

CHAPTER 3
POSITIONING YOURSELF

*You don't buy shares in IBM and show up
the next day to see if they need any help.*

This was my first experience of the next rung on the entrepreneurial ladder. Before that, all my focus had been staff and customers, the product, the proposition, and the team. These are, of course, the crucial elements in a start-up, but after start-up, they should all be the work of managers. Entrepreneurs get stuck in this mode.

Buying my second business changed everything. In particular, my conversations changed significantly. I no longer asked the operational questions: my conversations became more strategic. In fact, it led me to a conversation with Costco (at the time a $57 billion-a-year retailer), which had twenty-one shops across the UK. All of a sudden, I was pitching against the likes of Vodafone and other huge telecom companies. Within weeks, we had a pilot store within Costco, and soon after that, we started to roll out into other stores. This was a huge opportunity for a little telco, and I am convinced it came to me because I was creating better conversations. I had stopped acting like a hunter looking for sales and had started to play a bigger, more interesting game. This elicited a different conversation, one that showed that we were a successful telecom company that was looking to buy out others.

The Entrepreneur's Dilemma

Entrepreneurs thrive on change. We love it. It is why we chose our path. Our staff and our customers—not so much. What tends to happen is that every few months we reinvent everything and interfere in the business, usually after reading a particularly inspiring book or fresh off the back of a seminar (and probably right at the point where the last idea was just starting to gain some traction). So, what should an entrepreneur do? How do we scratch that itch?

If you position yourself as a shareholder in your business early on, you can start moving up the ladder and progressing as an entrepreneur. This is something that, had I known it earlier in my career, would have saved me a lot of time, effort, heartache, and headache.

It's only when you start thinking strategically about your business and, more importantly, talking more strategically, that you are exposed to new and very different opportunities. Everything starts to change once you position yourself as an investor. Your conversations with partners, clients, and contractors start to change. You see opportunities you didn't see before because you were too bogged down in the nitty-gritty.

In 2009, I bought an air-conditioning business for $1. On an angel investment website, I discovered a company seeking funds for their air-conditioning parts supply business. I arranged to meet with this company to potentially advise on raising capital for them. During our meeting, it was revealed that this entrepreneur had another completely separate air-conditioning company. This other company was in trouble. I found out that it had a lot of cash-flow problems. Bills were being paid in the wrong order, and, as a result, it meant the staff had not been paid in over two months. The staff were loyal and had been with the company for more than 20 years. The owner was in a tricky position: he was faced with closing the doors and not being able to pay his staff. His motivations were not to lose face with his employees while driving the new car he had purchased using money from his other business. I realized I could buy the business for $1, sort out the cash-flow issues, and sell it several months later.

Business Breakout: If It's Measured, It Improves

The metric you choose for your business tends to be the thing that gets better. It is where you put your focus. Most businesses focus on the profit and loss statement, so top-line and bottom-line improvement. But businesses don't fail from a lack of profits; they fail from a lack of cash. Cash really is king.

It is of first importance to understand where the cash is tied up in the balance sheet and then make your business metrics cash-related. Work with debtors, creditors, and stock. If you sell things with a margin, the rest will take care of itself. Remember the rules. Rule #1: More money coming in than going out. Rule #2: Always remember Rule #1.

Looking for the Signs

When someone is looking for money, find out why. Do they want you to pay off debts? Are they trying to fix a leaking bucket with more water? If they want you to invest in "the past," you are buying a losing lottery ticket. Focus on the future instead. In many cases, they wouldn't need money in the future if the past was fixed.

Deal Deep Dive: Paul and the Family Affair

Paul came to the Harbour Club in Mallorca in October 2017. After the course, he'd already done a few distressed deals when he came across an engineering company through a networking event contact.

After Paul had given his 30-second elevator pitch about being a business investor and during the open networking part of the event, he began to talk with a commercial mortgage broker. This broker told Paul that his next-door neighbor had had a turbulent time with a newly inherited business. She really wanted to sell. So, they set up a meeting.

Paul was introduced to Deb. She'd been happily married for just over ten years. Her husband, Keith, set up and ran a successful engineering business. Then, at the age of fifty-two, he unexpectedly passed away.

Paul said:

"So aside from the lessons that I learned about the business, this deal also taught me how not to write a will because he'd left 20% of his business to her and 80% to his two children from his first marriage. Then he'd left the family home, 80% to her and 20% to his two children."

Not having a clue about either engineering or running a business, Deb was thrust into a difficult situation. Before his death, Keith had been very much involved in running his business. He brought the business in, managed the customers, and ran the factory that made copper components for various industries. He died ten months before Paul met Deb. She had been trying to keep things afloat but, with no marketing, sales had started to decline. There was a good repeat order book that kept the family alive, and the business was still profitable, but if things had continued as they were, it wouldn't have been long before the business would have started to slip into a loss-making position.

The personal situation was much worse. Deb and the two children, aged seventeen and nineteen, didn't get along. She didn't have a high opinion of them either. The sons wanted her to put the house up for sale and move out, and for them to take their 20% when the property was sold. She wanted to keep the home where she was happy and enjoyed living there. She wanted to sell the business so that she could have a nest egg as she didn't have any other source of income.

The logical thing, of course, would've been for Deb and her sons to swap, whereby she would give them her 20% in the business in return for them giving up their 20% claim on the property, but they really didn't like each other or speak to each other. The atmosphere was quite difficult.

The business had revenues of about $2.24 million, and it was making about $260,000 profit. What interested Paul were the assets. The business owned its factory, which was worth about $460,000. The machinery to produce the copper components was worth about $330,000. There was a residential flat next door to the factory that was worth about $165,000. The children were living there rent-free, which annoyed Deb because they held wild parties there every weekend. The business had about $200,000 worth of cash in the bank and $100,000 worth of stock. So, despite its declining sales position, it still had some interesting assets. It was debt-free, and there was more than enough money in the bank for working capital, etc.

Paul had a good meeting with Deb and agreed to meet with the two sons. Their motivation was different in that they wanted her out of the house. They thought that the property was worth about $800,000, so their 20% would be worth about $80,000 each. They also recognized that they didn't have the experience to run the business. They wanted their dad's legacy to build the business back up to its more prosperous times so that then they could sell it, from which they could obviously benefit. They recognized that the business probably wasn't worth much at the time because, as a going concern, there was no leadership, no sales, and no customer service.

Paul did a deal whereby he took equity to resolve the problem. He prepared the business ready for sale, recruited to get the right people in place, and released some cash to give the sons something to play with. To resolve Deb's situation with the property so that she could still live there, he released some cash for her as well.

He structured the deal so that the sons, who wanted somewhere to live, were gifted the residential flat next door to the factory from the business. So, at the ages of 17 and 19, they now had a property of their own, mortgage-free. Paul gave them some cash out of the business account, $25,000 each, which attracted a corporation-tax liability. He then mortgaged the property to release some further cash. To get the mortgage, he needed to put a deposit of $90,000 down, which was taken out of the business account. What was left from the mortgage balance was used to pay Deb a lump sum to buy her shares out of the business and to leave some working capital in the business. Once all that was completed, Deb swapped her shares in the business for the shares in the property.

After doing the deal, Paul promoted the production manager to general manager to run the factory, including the job floor. He hired a sales engineer experienced in the industry who had developed trusted relationships. The plan was to get the business ready for sale, but Paul found working with the two sons was quite difficult. They were immature in their outlook, and their vision was different from Paul's.

Paul ended up selling his share of the business back to them for cash, some up front, some on deferral. He said:

"Now, I could've held it. I could've built the business. I could've sold it for more than I

did, but I think it would've been quite difficult working with them because of their different views and vision for the business.

"I learned how to use a company's assets to buy a stake in it. Because I felt a loyalty to the commercial mortgage broker for finding the deal in the first place, I used him to mortgage the commercial property to release the cash. In hindsight, I should have lined up a property investor prior to doing the deal who would have bought the building, maybe at a slight discount, and then leased it back. I wouldn't have required the $70,000 deposit to get the mortgage and would have still resulted in the same sort of cash result."

Paul learned a lot of lessons. He realized that, if he'd taken proper tax advice, he could have structured the company's cash differently to reduce the corporation tax liability. He might have been able to leverage more of the assets, like the machinery and the stock, which were worth a few hundred thousand dollars, to create enough cash to buy the sons outright. He said, "I would have owned 100% of the business, which would have given me the control and ability to do what I wanted to do with it."

Paul's gone on to do more than thirty deals since doing the Harbour Club course. Some have been simple; others more complex like this deal. He said, "The smallest deal I've done is $150,000 revenue business, and the largest is a $17.6 million revenue. I've also done a couple of mergers, and I'm currently in the process of building several agglomerations."

———

Part Two

Where You Find The Deals To Go Do

Everyone is looking for money,
so be what everyone is looking for.

A Note on Finding Good Businesses

To find a good target, it helps to know what you're looking for. You will have to learn how to consistently find good deals and keep the stream of deals flowing.

However, running a business is hard and all-consuming. If you don't commit everything to it, you will fail. Most do, but some make it through those early years and go on to be successful (by various measures).

Success doesn't make you immune to problems. Often, the businesses over-expand, or the owners take their eye off the ball, or there is a disruption in their industry or some macroeconomic event like a global financial crisis. Whatever the cause, companies are often slow to react. A bad month is just a bad month, but you don't need many bad months without "rightsizing" to totally wipe out your business. Your staff and your customers will assure you that it is business as usual, just a blip, and offer such comforting words as you glide gently to the scene of the crash. By the time you get there, it is often a case of too little, too late, or even enough, but too late.

Most of the really distressed companies I find are profitable on a 1-month snapshot, but the balance sheet is a mess. The creditors are lining up to give them a kick and the cash flow is a disaster. They are stuck in a spiral where, once they lose their credit rating or get a court judgment, then everyone else joins in the kicking. These people don't even think they can sell: "Who on earth will buy this?" They are sitting at home, depressed with a bottle of whiskey, when they should be on a business-for-sale website creating advertisements.

Then, at the other end of the spectrum, you have a decade-plus old business that generates seven figures a year of profit. The owners have a great culture, with their staff and their customers (their brand), and the business affords them a great lifestyle with holidays, probably a second home, maybe a boat. However, they are frustrated: they started this business to be the next Google or Apple, not a decent small company. They have probably tried to expand a few times in the past but have struggled to get through the glass ceiling. Most industries have a glass ceiling level, but just beyond it, they have to scale up their entire infrastructure and change the team dynamics.

You see, a company might be really profitable at $5 million of revenue, break even at $6 million, and start losing money at $7 million. They have to get to $10 million to get to the other side of the desert, but this can take some time. And all the while, they're bleeding; the holidays stop, the second home gets mortgaged, and eventually have to downsize and go back to being a great, profitable $5 million business. Then, after 2 or 3 years, it all seems like a good idea again. They think they've figured out how to break through this time, only to learn new lessons.

I often find company owners who have been through this cycle several times and are scratching their heads as to how to break through that glass ceiling. They would never dream of selling: it would be like selling a child. They want it to be everything they dreamt about when they started the thing in their bedroom.

We have the answer: they need to acquire their way to scale or join an agglomeration. (I'll discuss this in greater detail in Chapter 13.) But where to find these people if they are not for sale?

You need to learn how to consistently find good businesses, distressed or non-distressed, that are not for sale.

Get a Stream of Deals

A quick note on consistency and deal heat: I end up doing a deal with approximately one in ten of the companies that I pitch to. When Harbour Clubbers start, their success rate is more like one in twenty, although I have several members of my gold inner circle who are just as good as me and have multiple deals under their belts. It is not about finding a company; it is about finding a stream of companies. One common failure I see is that people start sourcing and then find an opportunity that appears to be moving forward, so they stop sourcing and focus all the attention on this one deal. If it works, wonderful, but, if it doesn't, they have no plan B, no more pipeline. They get despondent.

You need to keep working at the deal flow. If you have multiple deals all in discussion at the same time, you aren't perceived as desperate. That bit of blasé standoffishness will help get the deal done.

CHAPTER 4
DON'T SEEK BUSINESSES FOR SALE

Deals are everywhere—
tune in to "DEAL-FM" or look for the signs.

To find deals, you have to position yourself to be looking for deals in the first place. You have to think about where the deals are. It's tempting to google "businesses for sale," but all that will do is drag you down a rabbit hole to a bunch of brokers' websites or business-for-sale websites.

When you contact brokers, they have their own ideas concerning the deal structure and expected amounts of money. Tackling this mindset and getting them to change their minds can be both toxic and challenging. Brokers often manipulate the profit figures and then give the seller the idea that they can get huge multiples of the profit. Quite often, that's because the broker is charging an upfront fee. Their business is less about selling companies and more about signing up sellers to get these upfront fees.

Also, a company's broker selection is often dependent on who gave them the best deal. If two brokers say your business is worth $1 million, but another says it's worth $3 million, people don't tend to question where the other $2 million came from. They tend to sign up with the broker who tells them they can get $3 million. Invariably, the business sells for $1 million, but the broker still gets their commission: they inflated the price to get the company on board. Sometimes it takes a year for somebody to realize this—and sometimes it takes them five or six years.

Property experts don't spend their days staring into real estate agents' windows. You should not be looking for bankruptcy attorneys, business-for-sale websites, or business brokers. If you are looking to acquire a business, don't look for businesses for sale. The reasons are many, but here are a few:

1. **You are probably dealing with a broker:** Not always, but with a lot of businesses that are actively selling, you end up dealing with a broker. The broker can't make a decision. Their primary interest is in getting the highest price because, in addition to their upfront fee, they receive a percentage of the deal. You want to deal directly with the principals in order to build rapport. This makes it possible for you to understand their motivations and needs. This understanding makes it possible for you to present a deal structure that solves their issues and gets you a deal: the win-win scenario.

2. **You can get into a competitive bid situation:** Here, you are being played against another buyer (real or imaginary). The fact that the owners are actively selling can create huge time traps, whereby you invest weeks or even months of your time only to find out they had a cash buyer all along and just wanted you as a stalking horse.

3. **High expectations:** The seller's better half is down at the Mercedes showroom, picking out the leather colors. Try and talk them down from that one.

4. **Mentally checked-out:** Businesses frequently decline in the year after they are put up for sale because the owner has mentally checked out. Businesses take nine to eighteen months to sell the conventional way (just the physical process), even when you have a buyer ready. Deal fatigue can set in, affecting the business. This then means that at the last minute, the buyer wants a better price for the now smaller business.

5. **Who will run it?** Don't buy a job. A business for sale often means the manager who has been running it for years (often massively underpaid) is leaving, and you will need to jump into their shoes—which means you end up with a full-time job. What's more, if you do a leveraged buy-out (LBO) and borrow money to do the deal, you not only have a full-time job but all the money from that job goes to the bank for the next five or seven years, assuming the business stays the same or grows. If it shrinks, the bank takes your house. Joy!

6. **Manipulated accounts (optimized, if I'm being generous):** When businesses are being sold, it's amazing how good the prior financial year—just before they sell—is compared to the previous eighteen! And, of course, next year will be the best ever. It is also common (especially if there is a broker) to add back expenses to inflate the profits and then multiply the profits up. For instance, they might say they are selling at five or six times earnings, but they have added back their salary, the interest charges from the bank, the coffee machine, half the phone bill and anything else they can find that they wish they hadn't bought (but did). The premise being that you won't incur these costs, so these are the true underlying profit. Well, you

can't blame them for trying! Any savings you can make are your upside. If they wish they had run the business differently, well then, they should have run the thing differently!

7. **Reading too much TechCrunch:** You always get the people who decide they want to sell something and create this "amazing" brand/culture/ product—so amazing that it generates sales of $100,000 a year and is somehow worth gazillions of dollars. A little naivety and reading too much TechCrunch are all that is needed to massively inflate the ego and price tag of an ordinary business. Find a seasoned entrepreneur who's had a few more trips around the block in their career.

8. **Bankruptcy Attorneys:** Too late—it's like a doctor looking for patients in a graveyard. If you are looking for a distressed deal, you want the guy who's thinking of calling the bankruptcy attorney, because after they do, it's dead. Most likely, everyone has lost their jobs, creditors won't get paid, and clients will be left high and dry. If you can get in before all this happens, you can rescue it. Of course, insolvency may form part of a wider strategy, but it's not a source of deals. It's a tool, not a market.

So, what can you do?

Network

Networking can be hugely powerful. There are plenty of organized networking events specifically designed to do business. Try going to one of these and saying you are an investor. You will get everyone's business cards immediately. You just have to weed out the real estate deals and start-ups to get to the real businesses.

But it doesn't have to be the structured kind of networking. Every meeting, dinner date, or coffee break could be a new opportunity. You have hundreds of contacts saved in your phone, and none of them know you are an investor in SMEs. Why not make a list of thirty and call them all for a chat?

Start by asking if you can help them. I call this the karmic deficit: help them, and they will feel compelled to help you. So, is there an introduction you can make or is some other way to support them? Then say what you are looking for and see if they can help. This exercise is also hugely useful for you to be comfortable with what you say and how you deal with common questions. After the thirtieth call, you will sound like a pro and are ready to be dropped straight into a live-fire scenario!

You also need to learn to look for the signs. Our brains have powerful filters that ignore everything "non-core." You need to tune into deal opportunities. It sounds simple, but most people don't listen. They are just waiting to say what they want to say next. If you listen, you will find deals everywhere in everyday conversations.

Andrew, who did the first Harbour Club course back in 2009, went on vacation right afterward and ended up buying a lighting manufacturing business from a lady he met at a dinner party. A week before, it would have just been an interesting conversation with a person who moaned a bit about their business, but because Andrew was tuned in, he found a deal.

There are deals everywhere if you listen differently. At the Harbour Club, you will learn this important skill of applying a filter to how you listen. Your next deal is likely already in your cell phone.

Identify as an Investor

The one thing everybody is looking for is money. If you have the thing that everybody is looking for, you'll have more conversations than anybody else. By positioning yourself as an investor when you go to networking meetings or even to a dinner party, you'll find that conversations open up to you that perhaps you didn't see previously. It's a bit like tuning in to a "DEAL-FM" radio station. As soon as you position yourself as an investor, many people will want to talk to you about how they can get that money from you.

Every dollar you'll ever make is in somebody else's pocket right now. Being an investor is like putting up a big sign saying, "I've got dollars in my pocket, and if you're smart enough, you can get them off me." That starts many interesting conversations.

A good thing about these conversations is that the people you're talking to tend to be straight with you. Of course, everybody is going to put a positive spin on things. Still, they're not going to tell you they have a $10 million revenue company if they have a $2 million revenue company because they know that, as an investor, you're going to look under the hood at some point. If they get caught, then the deal is off. You'll actually start some slightly more honest conversations about things.

You'll find that the first thing you need to identify is what they would spend the money on, and that will help you categorize whether this is a start-up business or whether it's a business that's established and already operating. That is a helpful distinction. In the Harbour Club, we have two focus areas.

Focus 1: Tactical, Distressed, or Bolt-on Acquisitions

These acquisitions tend to be smaller companies that you're targeting because they're distressed, or you're using them as a bolt-on to grow your existing business by increasing either the products and services that you offer or perhaps to get some key talent or clients that exist in that business. This is a tactical move: you're adding something that you don't currently have.

These businesses seem to have a sweet spot, between about $500,000 and $5 million in top-line revenue. Below $500,000 in top-line revenue, you will find they are likely to be either owner-centric or one-customer-centric—they're all built around what one person does, or they're all built around one customer's contribution. That means responsibilities haven't been assigned in the usual way, so you've got key person risk. Obviously, if they're one-customer-focused, you've got key client risk—but when they get to about $40,000 a month, these are the sorts of issues that tend to be resolved.

There are always exceptions to the rule, but generally speaking, above the $5 million top-line revenue level, a business has started to delineate responsibilities. Marketing and finance have been given to two different people, which is great. (If you've ever seen accounts done by a marketing person, you'll understand.) The management tends to have gotten away from that one-customer thing by productizing their business. They've got an offering and a pricing structure that's scalable. That $500,000—$5 million range is a good guide for a tactical, bolt-on, distressed type of deal.

Focus 2: Strategic Acquisitions

Strategic acquisitions are for when you want to enter a new market or new territory—for example, you want an office in Indonesia or a different geographical part of your own country, or you're looking for an order-of-magnitude acquisition. Typically, in the Harbour Club, we focus on companies that are profitable and have a history of generating profit, not the one-hit-wonder that has just become profitable.

Instead of $500,000 to $5 million of revenue, it's $500,000 to $5 million of *profit* that these companies are generating. They're typically debt-free. We don't like a bank or financial institution to have some kind of lien or charge over the business because you'll often find that they have a lot of control. If you have a bad year, it can suddenly be your last year. It's always good to add a nice debt-free business to the group.

In these situations, the management is usually staying. These are businesses where you want to be a shareholder or a business owner, not a business runner. You want to be the shareholder, not the director managing the people. It's important that you behave as a shareholder in these situations. The way I often describe it is that you wouldn't buy shares in IBM and then arrive the next day to see if they needed any help with anything. You wait for your regular reports, and you complain vehemently if they're not what you were expecting. You need to get into that kind of shareholder mentality with those bigger, more profitable businesses. Otherwise, you're creating a mammoth job for yourself.

Business Breakout: Rebranding Obsession

Don't let your ego get in the way of your success. Many people want to buy one or more companies and then rebrand, getting them all under one name. There's almost no good reason for this other than to satisfy your ego. I have seen businesses that have created a niche under their name for twenty years and have then been bought and given a new name thought up in a boardroom a few weeks before, because the board wanted to create a unified brand or message for customers. Don't bother—it's a waste of time, money and effort, confusing for both customers and staff. It adds zero value. Also, in the first few months, you are likely to make changes, changes can create problems, and so all those problems then get associated with the new brand.

It's All About Rapport

When you do a deal with an owner-managed business, it's different from anything you might have learned about M&A strategies, particularly if you've considered the traditional corporate finance route or the MBA way. When you're dealing with an owner-manager, it's all about rapport, creating a relationship with them, and then doing a deal together that meets some common aim. It needs to be a win-win deal. You are solving a problem for them, and you're getting the business as a result of solving that problem.

Buying a business is often positioned as a procurement process. It's *buying*, therefore, it's procurement. Procurement is about picking holes, finding faults, looking for issues, doing your due diligence, negotiating like a used car salesman where you mutter under your breath as soon as they tell you how much they want for the business.

But when you're dealing with owner-managed businesses, it's more of a collaborative approach. The key is to focus on what you're bringing to the party, which means not thinking of it as a procurement process.

I get this, my Harbour Club alumni get it, and that's why we are able to do so many more deals in this SME space. We understand that key differentiation. People want to do deals with us because we're solving their problem—even if we haven't put the most cash on the table. We've created rapport and a situation in which the deal can happen.

In fact, we often take deals from right under the noses of other buyers who are offering more but are bogged down in the procurement process. Many years ago, a friend of mine, who has since done the Harbour Club course, called me to tell me that he had found a company that had been going through a sales process for six months and getting "deal fatigue." He said he felt like it was a deal I could do in an afternoon, so I went into a joint venture with him, and within a week, we had bought the business. Interestingly, we then had two possible buyers, and the one we actually sold to was the one who had been messing about for six months!

Buying is Selling

Buying a business is a sales process. Look at any book on sales: it will discuss building credibility, building rapport, understanding the customer's needs, identifying the needs, selling the benefits, and closing. All those factors in a sales process actually work (and are even essential) in the "buying a business" process. This means that if you're looking to buy a company, sourcing is marketing. If Sales is signing up the people who've got their hands in the air, Marketing is getting people to put their hands up. We need to find a way to achieve this.

Most businesspeople are naturally good at a few different ways of marketing to customers. Some people are natural networkers. Stick them in a room full of people, and they'll have everybody's business cards by the end of the meeting and three people scheduled for a follow-up coffee or beer. Put somebody else in that same room, and they'll grab one person, stick them in a corner and talk at them relentlessly for the whole evening, not really interested in whether or not it turns into any kind of business.

The same goes for telephone sales. Some people are natural at building rapport on the phone and can even do a whole deal on the phone. Other people just can't close on the phone. Some people are great at online marketing. There are all sorts of different ways to find a customer, so focus on what you're good at. Position yourself as an investor, then use the method that suits you best to get potential inquiries. Get yourself into your strongest position.

One of the strategies that work well at the Harbour Club is letter writing, which we'll talk about later in the book. It's not really about being able to write a letter and stuff it in an envelope; it's about what you do with the inquiry. Some people are naturally good at dealing with the inbound traffic—the people who respond to those letters. Others just can't turn them into meaningful conversations.

One of our Harbour Club alumni sent out loads of letters and received loads of interested incoming calls, but none of them turned into a deal. He decided to walk into the offices of one of the companies and go and see the guy face to face. He walked in, met with the right person, and ended up doing a deal with them. Clearly, his forte was in that kind of face-to-face situation.

I remember that when I first moved to Mallorca from the UK, I had an inquiry from somebody who contacted me through LinkedIn, where I'm positioned as an investor. I was desperately trying to avoid flying to the UK immediately to do this deal. I decided for the first time to diverge from my own process (i.e., a fact-finding call, go away and work out the deal, then go back and do a face-to-face meeting). I tried doing the deal over the phone. I was amazed: it took about two weeks to close the deal remotely, and I'd never met the person, or even been to their office. I'd done everything over the phone, including closing the deal. (Of course, I then owned this business, which was in the UK, so eventually I had to go back to do the turnaround part of the equation.)

I took this a step further with an online retailing business in Essex that I was able to buy and sell without ever setting foot on the premises. I did the deal over the phone, found a buyer, and sold it remotely. I did have a joint-venture associate on the ground who went in to do some of the turnaround part. It was an experiment to see if it was possible.

Break Your Deal Virginity

The most important deal is your first deal. When I closed my first deal, it represented a year's worth of sales in an afternoon. It was a hugely powerful addition to my business. It also gave me a story to tell about how I now owned a telecom company that bought businesses. This narrative led me into my second deal and my third deal, and I haven't looked back since. You get wonderful lessons from every deal that you do: you learn what you're going to do next time.

Deal Deep Dive: The
Optimized Clinic Accounts

A Harbour Club delegate shows me a deal. He meets the potential clients through networking, but they have already appointed a broker. The business is a chain of clinics for sale in London, established for twenty years, with £1.3 million in annual gross revenue and £250,000 profit. They want a deal for £300,000 cash up front, and they're happy to have the balance as some sort of earn-out or deferred payment. On the face of it, fine, back to black in just over a year, yes? No.

A quick look at Companies House (the UK's registrar of companies) revealed that the profit is "adjusted;" it was really a loss of £65,000 for the year. The broker had added things back to the P&L that the business wished it hadn't bought in order to get to the inflated profit number. Added to that, the company has a who's who of finance companies (seven different ones in all) to whom they owe a total of £300,000.

This is not a normal deal. We will offer a no-money-down deal. I can see a quick £100,000 savings, which would make them profitable, but I am now fighting the business owner's expectation of £300,000 of cash that has been planted by a broker. They may go ahead, or they may take years to realize that no one will give them the money, or they may actually fail. We will see!

———————

CHAPTER 5
FOCUS ON MOTIVATIONS, NOT MONEY

Simply changing your conversations to be more
strategic places you in a very different space.

If you're not looking for a business that's for sale, what are you looking for? You're looking for somebody who has motivations. They have a problem they need to solve. There's something that's not right with their business that needs fixing, but they haven't thought about selling it as an approach to resolving the issue.

Their motivation may be that they're completely distressed and can't make the payroll at the end of the month. They might not be getting what they wanted out of the business, or they're not enjoying life enough. They could be ill, or their relatives are ill, and they want to spend more time with them and less time in the office. They are motivated. You need to identify the motivation first, then look at the deal from that angle. It's about really listening and asking the right questions, as they will probably say everything is wonderful and they just need money. Don't take that at face value; keep digging until you get to the real issue.

If you are looking to buy a business that is seeking investment, you should ask why it is looking for capital. Perhaps you can meet the motivations without cash. Let me illustrate this with an example I worked on a few years ago. I found a training business based in the UK, but with foreign owners.

1. The company was profitable, with revenues of £3.5 million.
2. On the downside, the accounts were a shambles, and they had not been accounting for sales tax properly.
3. The owners had also lent the company over £100,000 to support cash flow, but it was periodically asking for more, putting pressure on their domestic businesses' cash flow.
4. A major supplier was threatening to stop deliveries because of non-payment and a strained relationship with the management.

They wanted someone to pay off their loan and give them some cash for the business. That may have been what they were saying, but it was not what they needed.

By listening to them, I realized they just wanted this thing off their plate and were at a loss as to how to achieve this without feeling as if they were giving the business away. (Who wants to part with the dusty painting only to find out it was a Picasso?!) I was able to take a controlling stake (60% in this case), resolve the problems with the supplier, sort out the cash-flow issue—which was all down to a bad deal with their credit card processor—and sort out their accounts so that they were tax compliant. This is what they needed: a local partner and no more headaches from their overseas venture.

Business Breakout: Gaining Control

On the topic of controlling stakes, at the Harbour Club, we teach you how to gain a controlling stake without taking the technical majority of 51% or the majority rule stake of 76%. We have a methodology where we can take any stake or percentage and gain control of everything.

It is far more important to focus your energies on an in-depth understanding of motivations than on the asking price. In another example, I managed to secure the controlling stake of a $12 million company with no capital. Harbour Club delegates are doing this all the time.

Forget About Price—It's All About Structure

People get so bogged down about price that they forget that they can build a structure that will enable them to buy the business without using any capital and without borrowing any money. If you can de-risk at the beginning, then effectively, it's all upside. The best way to protect your wealth and protect yourself is to cover your downside. If you always do deals with no downside, you can never really get stuck. The only costs are opportunity costs. You waste a bit of time, and that's pretty much it. I tell my Harbour Club members that if you buy a business for $1, you can eBay the doormat and there's your profit! It's all upside from here.

Don't worry so much about the price: focus on the structure. A great example is Jim, one of the men who did the Harbour Club course. He had met business owners in the past and had talked to some of them about buying them. However, he was stuck in the traditional kind of procurement process approach—in other words, you ask them how much they want for their business and, whatever figure they say, you try to haggle them down. They say they want $1.2 million, you say $600,000, and then you argue. You end up either annoying them and not getting the business at all or getting the business at a bit of a discount but having to come up with all the money up front to buy it.

A disarming way of approaching these conversations is to agree with people. It's the old Dale Carnegie How to Win Friends and Influence People method. Even when people say something that you don't like, you start by agreeing with them and then work back to how you get to where you want to be.

Deal Deep Dive: Here's the Deal that We've Got on the Table

After learning about the "win friends and influence" tactic at the Harbour Club, Jim went off looking for another deal. He ignored two of the Harbour Club general guidelines—don't look for companies for sale and avoid retirement sales (because they can be tricky and fixated on getting all cash up front)—and went to talk to a 72-year-old man who wanted to retire and was trying to sell his business.

The man had the business up for sale for two years. It was a good little business. It was making $395,000 a year in profit, had $525,000 in the bank, and owned its own property. This was a small industrial site where the company was the main tenant. A third of the site was rented out to another tenant who paid a healthy rent. The site was valued at around $1.3 million. The man wanted $1.6 million for the business, which is not at all greedy. It was like getting the business for free with the property and the cash in the bank. You're pretty much being paid to take it away.

He'd been advertising it through the usual channels, online and everywhere else, and everybody who approached him had taken the $1.6

million figure and tried to negotiate. He believed he was asking for a realistic figure, not being greedy; he just wanted to retire with a bit of cash. But everyone was trying to low-ball him and offer him less money. The Harbour Clubber just went in there and said, "Okay, we'll pay you $1.6 million; how do we get you to your $1.6 million." And then he structured a deal that was basically self-financing.

Jim gave the retiree the cash in the bank, leaving enough behind for some working capital. Jim also gave him a deferred payment, paying him some money over a 12- to 18-month period that would effectively be paid for from the profits of the company. He also released some cash from selling the property. In this particular scenario, he sold the property to his own pension, creating a self-invested pension plan and released $525,000 of cash from the sale. Jim then had $1 million of property sitting in his pension with only a $525,000 mortgage against it, which is how it was financed. Of course, it was a self-invested pension plan mortgage, so it was the pension company's responsibility, not his personal responsibility: he could have sold the property and leased it back with an investor as an alternative.

Jim gave the retiree this simple structure: a bit of your own cash now, a bit of cash over time, and a bit of cash released from the property. That gets you to your $1.6 million, and then you get to walk away with exactly what you want.

The retiree had been trying to sell the business for two years. Now here was an opportunity to get the money he wanted. The only headwind he had was his daughter and his accountant, who were advising him not to do the deal because Jim wasn't putting any of his own money in.

How did Jim overcome the objection? That came down to a rapport-building exercise. Jim spent lots of time with the man, making sure he got to know Jim properly and see that he was genuine and wanted to do the deal. Jim showed him he was to be trusted. He also reminded him that he wouldn't want to spend another two years not selling the business! Did the retiree really want to sit there for another two years trying to find somebody who would pay them the full amount in cash up front? The net result was the deal got done, and it was the right deal to get done.

———————

CHAPTER 6
CAPITALIZE ON BAD PAYERS

You can't fix a leaking bucket with more water.

W hat follows is a useful process for locating and communicating with distressed companies. A word of warning: you need to know what you are doing. This is a powerful tool for finding distressed companies, but remember you need to know how to acquire them safely and turn them around, or you can be messing with people's lives.

The legal definition of insolvency is being "unable to meet your debts when they become due." Anyone not paying on time and without an arrangement to pay is insolvent in the eyes of the law, and one is not allowed to trade when knowingly insolvent. On that basis, there are a lot of companies that are technically insolvent. A business is not permitted to operate when it's knowingly insolvent, and the directors can become personally liable for the debts of the company. It's a serious, major issue.

The key is to find people when they are in trouble, but before they call the bankruptcy attorney, who will, by the way, ruin everything for the staff, the creditors, the customers, and the owner. It is a race to get there first and save the day.

Here's the overview of the tactic:

1. Start with companies that supply products or services to businesses and find out who is on their "naughty list" (i.e., who is a bad payer).
2. Search for those people on a credit-checking tool, such as Hoovers or Dunn & Bradstreet.
3. Make sure they are not some huge multinational company (also bad payers apparently) and fit our acquisition profile.[1]
4. Write a letter as an investor to each of the directors at their director's service address (usually their home). We have played around with this quite a bit and the right letter to the right companies can get you a high percentage of results.

The home address part is key. It can also be used for geographical or sector targeting. The letter can't come from a business, so don't include a logo. It mustn't look like a marketing activity or any kind of "mass production" letter. It needs to be a personal letter from you to them.

I cannot count how many deals have been found this way. Lee, who did the Harbour Club course for a second time, recently told me he had done eight deals, with 100% of them coming from the letter strategy. The Harbour Club alumni send out thousands of these kinds of letters and get incredible response rates. But you need to be able to properly deal with the phone responses. There's a massive difference between people who are having success with this strategy and people who aren't.

---

1 Ideally (but you can bend the rules here), an acquisition profile will have more than $500,000 in revenue, be geographically accessible, or have a partner nearby (you can guarantee that the further away it is, the more you will need to be there!), and it will be owner-managed or have only a small number of shareholders (two or three).

And it all seems to be about how they achieve rapport on the phone when they get an inquiry.

Those Who Call Get to Ask All the Questions

The people who are really good at striking up a chatty conversation and building rapport on the phone are getting deals, and the people who aren't comfortable with that aren't getting them. There is a basic piece of telephone etiquette—the person who calls gets to ask all the questions.

When you send one of these letters, what tends to happen is that people call you. And when they call you, they want to ask you all sorts of questions like, "Where did you get my details," "How much money have you got," and "What sort of businesses have you invested in before?" And they start going down all these different rabbit holes, which basically means that you can't direct the conversation, as you would like to do.

My suggestion is that you start by making an excuse. When they call, tell them your doorbell just rang and you have to answer it, or whatever you want to say you're doing. Then arrange a time to call them back when they've got fifteen minutes of free time. You might be on the phone with them for a couple of hours but tell them that, and you'll scare them off. Tell them you need fifteen minutes of their undivided attention to go through a few things with them. And then make that call back to them. Then, because you called them, you get to ask all the questions. You can say, "Have you always been a widget manufacturer?" "Was your father a widget manufacturer?" "When did you manufacture your first widget?" This way, you can start drilling down into the nuts and bolts about them and their business and get a good understanding of what's going on.

Then, of course, once you've built some rapport by asking open questions and listening, you can start to dive into some of the trickier questions about their finances, their creditors, what's going on in the business. If they want an investment from you, what are they going to spend it on? How are they going to deploy the cash? Is it for fixing old problems? You need to find out if you're buying the losing lottery ticket. Or do they want to invest in something new? Why do they need that investment for something new? This approach will give you a much better understanding of the business and where it is financially. If you dive straight into the financials without building the rapport, they will clam up and not tell you anything. I've even had situations where people won't say their company name, even when you know their company name or won't divulge basic financial information, which you can see on online public records. But once you've built the rapport, they'll tell you everything you want to know and more.

Rapport is essential, but this is a strategy that suits certain people more than others.

Deal Deep Dive: The Only Interesting Thing in the Post?

I'd done my first couple of deals and was starting to get a reputation for myself as somebody who could complete deals. Then an acquaintance referred a telecom company in Kent in the UK to me. They hadn't been paying their bills on time.

I sat, wondering how I would reach out to them. If I called them up and said, "Hi, I hear you're in loads of trouble," I didn't think that would work as a great conversation starter. I pondered for a while.

In my telecom company, we had just bought new credit-checking software. Whenever we had a new telecom client, we were able to check their credit-worthiness, whether they had any court judgments against them, how long the business had been going for, all that kind of information. Of course, I credit checked everyone I'd ever met—all my friends, all the companies I dealt with. I typed in this company name and thought I'd have a quick look at them. I could see they were six years old, with $660,000 of annual gross revenue, which would be a nice addition to my business. Then I spotted that all the director's names were listed, each with their service address. I realized this meant I could write to the directors, perhaps via their accountant, or in some cases, to their home address.

I still didn't know what I'd put in the letter other than, "Hey, I know you're in trouble...," so I figured I'd focus on investment.

I wrote a vague, badly worded letter along the lines: "Hey, are you looking for an investor? Or are you looking to sell your business? Or are you looking to merge?"

It's pretty similar to the letter we use right up to this day, because the response rates—particularly from a direct mail perspective—are really good. They're incredible response rates.

I wrote the letters on a busy Friday afternoon, planning to drop them in the mailbox on the way home. At about 6:45 pm, when the sorting office at the post office would be closing in fifteen minutes, I grabbed the letters, shot down to the sorting office, and slammed them into the letterbox. Then I went to meet the rest of the team down in the local pub. After God knows how many gin and tonics, I woke up the next day at home to my phone ringing. I answered the phone, and this guy says, "Hi, I got your letter."

It was instant gratification. I wondered if the postman had taken that letter straight to the man on purpose! I realized it was really powerful for a number of reasons:

1. It was written from me to them. I hadn't put it on a corporate letterhead. I'd just put, "From Jeremy, to Dave." That personal approach helped and really resonated.
2. I mentioned investment. While too many people try and fill the leaking bucket with more water, it's true that everybody is looking for money to try and fix their problem. If everybody is looking for money, why don't you position yourself as offering

what everybody's looking for as a conversation starter? Have honest conversations with people about their business and what their plans are. Let's face it, if it's a really good investment, you will invest money—but it probably isn't, so maybe you will invest your most precious commodity: time.

3. I wrote to the directors at their home addresses, not their main business address. When mail comes to the main business address, it piles up, gets thrown away, or forwarded to different departments. When you write to somebody at their home address, they read it. Direct mail is a dying art. Apart from a few bills, your letter will probably be the only interesting thing in their mailbox that week.

Now, this particular response didn't turn into a deal. I hope it wasn't the hangover. You know you have to kiss a few frogs to find your prince or princess, but what it taught me was how to reach out to a potential target in a highly effective way. It also makes them take a step toward you, and this really helps. We have had many Harbour Clubbers who call all the people they send letters to, and they do have more meetings than not, but they also don't appear to do more deals. I think this idea that both sides each take a step toward the other is really powerful.

———————

Part Three

How You Do The Deals

Solving a business's problems with cash is like giving candy to children—it's a bad idea and they come back for more.

A Note on Structuring Deals

So, now you have an idea why you would do deals and how you can get in touch with those opportunities. What next? You need to know how to structure a win-win deal without getting stuck in the "cash up front" paradigm. In this chapter, we will give you some tried and tested tools from the Harbour Club on how to actually get the deal done.

I will also go through a typical process from inquiry to meeting the staff as the new owner. The steps in the process have been used frequently to capture as many of the possible targets as possible. You need to maximize the frogs to prince/princess ratio.

CHAPTER 7
THE APPROACH

Deals are like concrete—the longer
you leave them, the harder they get.

The approach is a fact-finding mission. It's important for you to gather information about the business so that you can think about the ideal structure to use. Then you go and present this deal structure to them.

The process boils down to the initial phone call, which is a big fact-finding phone call and rapport-building exercise in gathering information and how you can fix the business, then having a face-to-face meeting. Let's run through that process now, because it's quite different from other kinds of normal M&A situations.

Initial Phone Call

Let's say you've sent them the letter (there are many other ways you may have reached out to them: email, they call you, etc.). It's important that you set a telephone date, where you're going to call them back, so say to them, "Look, is there a good time when I can speak to you when you're going to have ten to fifteen minutes uninterrupted, and we can go through everything to do with the business?"

Remember the basic bit of telephone etiquette? "Those who call get to ask all the questions." If they call, they'll start rattling off loads of questions to you, so it's vital to control the call.

Fact-Finding Call and Rapport Building

You have to focus on rapport, not just questioning them relentlessly. Obviously, there will be loads of things you'd love to know about the business. What's its gross annual revenue? Profit? What are the big challenges they're facing? What are their liabilities, and who are the creditors that are pressing for their money? How much do they owe in taxes? All these things are wonderful to find out but, if you start diving into that kind of nitty-gritty at the beginning, you might find that all the defenses go up and people get really uncomfortable.

Spend as much time as possible just building rapport. Get to understand what their journey has been, how they developed this business, what their upbringing was like. Whenever you're speaking to people like this, you can always find mutual ground of shared experiences. Contribute your own experiences. Get to know them as a person. Build rapport and trust, so you can start to find out some of the business particulars. It's much easier for them to share that information with you because the skepticism has been considerably reduced.

I often ask the question, "If you could wave a magic wand that solved all your problems, what would that look like?" You want to find out whether they understand what it takes to get away from where they are now.

Although I always say, "When do you have ten to fifteen minutes to spare?" it's not unusual for these fact-finding calls to go on for a couple of hours—you really do get into the person's life story. This is valuable time, as this rapport is incredibly important to the transaction.

By the end of the call, you should have all the information that you need to be able to make the decision on how a transaction might look in terms of the kind of deal structures that we're talking about. When the call finishes, you say that you're going to consider the information and you'll be back in touch. The ball is in your court.

Deliberate, Think, and Come Up with a Plan

In the Harbour Club group, people usually share their questions with the other members, "Hey, what would you do?" "What do you think about this?" "Do you think I should do it this way or that way?" Sometimes they ask me about the opportunity, and I'll agree or point out a different way to do it. This thinking time is incredibly valuable. Having a group of peers you can talk to, and who have gone through deals that might be similar, will help you formulate the best plan for you and the business.

Once you've got an idea of a deal structure in your head and you've decided how you're going to approach the transaction, you then need to consider the things you could do quickly to re-establish the "more money coming in than going out" principle I covered earlier. We always try and focus on things you can take away, not things you can add. So, instead of thinking of how you can get more sales or more leads, can you fix the business with fewer overheads or no bank debt, for example? "Takeaways" are much easier than "adds." Unfortunately, entrepreneurs are always over-confident in their ability to add to the business, so you have to recognize this weakness, try to ignore it, and focus on the tangible savings that can be made.

Now you have two parts to the plan—the deal and the post-deal.

Face to Face

The next step is the face-to-face meeting. As I've said earlier, I've done deals over the phone, but, particularly when you're starting out, nothing beats a face-to-face. Even now, after all the deals I've done, nothing beats it.

Arrange the face-to-face meeting, ideally at the potential client's place. Go in and actually see the business. Sometimes they're reluctant to let people into the building in case the staff gets wind of what's going on, but I can't believe that any business never has visitors, so it would be sheer paranoia on their part to have you meet somewhere else. I have had the occasional situation where I have had to meet them after everyone's gone home in the evening, or at a café around the corner, but, ideally, meet at the business premises.

At this first meeting, even though you built telephone rapport, you now need to build face-to-face rapport. You have to start again, go back through everything, listen to them repeating themselves, and telling you all the same stories they told you on the phone. You have to grin and bear it and go back through that process of building rapport.

These first face-to-face meetings can last a long time. Once you've drilled down into understanding what their needs and issues are, you can present a solution to their problems there and then. Present them with a deal structure that will solve the biggest problem they have in their life right at that moment.

Then you close. You present your deal structure, and you say, "I'm ready to go ahead. We can do this right now." You're basically saying, "The only thing holding up fixing the biggest problem you have in your life is you, because I'm giving you the solution, and I'm ready to go."

Now, shut up.

You need to let the idea percolate through their brains, and for them to understand the gravity of what you've just said, because they're probably going through a Groundhog Day thing. They've probably met with people who've talked about investing in their business or talked about doing something to solve the problem. They've been lovely meetings. Everyone's nodding and laughing, but then the person goes away, and nothing happens. That's the typical outcome of these meetings, and they've been doing them again and again, getting more desperate as they go along.

You've massively interrupted the mental pattern they have for these kinds of meetings. They have a framework that their brains are following, of how these meetings are supposed to go. They're not supposed to go in a way where the solution to their problem is presented in the meeting, right there and then. So, it may take them a little while before they say something.

There's an old sales saying, "He or she who talks first loses." You need to keep your mouth shut, wait for them, and let one of them be the first person to speak.

They will probably say something like, "Well, don't you need to do some due diligence?" or, "I need to discuss it with my lawyer," or "I need to discuss it with my partner, or the guy down at the pub." There's always an objection. Let them voice the objection first. Don't try and put words in their mouth. The objection will be something around the topic of, "I need to think about it."

The Most Powerful Thing You Can Say

If the objection is due diligence with a distressed company, say:

"Look, I don't think we've got time to do a full due diligence because, by the time we finish that, A, there may no longer be a business and B, we *know* this business has problems. It's clearly not paying its creditors, so there's a high risk that it's not viable as a going concern and that it's trading insolvently. We need to get in as quickly as possible and find out what's going on, and I

think if we mess around doing due diligence, we won't be able
to do that. I'm going to look you in the eye and just trust you,
and shake hands and get on with this thing, because otherwise,
I don't think there's going to be anything left for us to fix."

That's a hugely powerful statement because you're saying, "Look, I
just trust you implicitly, and I want to help." Of course, you are buying
a limited liability company with another limited liability company, and
any trouble that it is in, or any trading that's happened while it's been
insolvent, has all been on their watch. So, actually, you're not really
taking any risk at all.[2] You are in a pretty strong position.

You might be thinking, "Well, do you need to do due diligence?' Of
course, but do the due diligence when you're already in there and are the
owner. Get the staff to go through the full due diligence process. You'll
need all this information when it comes to selling the business anyway.
Plus, this is an opportunity to take a deep dive into the business to get a
clear understanding of everything that goes on.

There are a number of advantages to this. For starters, you
already have the business, so there's no them and us when it comes to
communication with the team. You don't have to pay for it, so you're not
paying a third party to come in and do the due diligence. You're doing
it internally, within the business, using their staff and your guidance.
So, effectively, it doesn't cost you anything, and it saves a bucket load
of time.

It also saves the vendor a lot of embarrassment. Look, they know the
business is in trouble. They don't need somebody to come in and poke
around for four or five weeks and then tell them what they already know.
It doesn't help the situation, and it's certainly not good for rapport.

---

2   Of course, there is no such thing as no risk, but the use of limited liability is
     very helpful at reducing the financial risk—always seek legal advice for your own
     situation.

We say that we're going to trust them and we're going to get on with the deal.

They Want to Think About It

The primary objection that normally comes out in these situations is, "I want to think about it." They might need to speak to somebody else, or they genuinely need to think about it. It's rare that businesses do the deal on the day.

When they say they want to think about it, it's tempting to say "Okay" and run out the door. This is where you really need to hold onto your nerve and say:

> "Okay, but let's at least leave you with something to think about. Let's draw up a basic term sheet, a simple letter of agreement between us that you've contributed to and I've contributed to, that sets out what this deal is exactly. So that when you're thinking about it, or when you're discussing it with your partner, at least you've clearly written down exactly what's going to happen. Otherwise, when you're trying to articulate it, you're not going to know the nitty-gritty of what's going to be agreed on."

Avoid the Problems with Legal Agreements

Then we do something different: instead of leaving and emailing an agreement, we drag our chair to their side of the desk. If you literally move the chair to their side of the desk, metaphorically, you show you're on their side. Position yourself shoulder to shoulder with them, trying to solve the problem that's in front of you both. Use the same computer to draft this agreement together.

It's important that they have input into the agreement as well as you. You start by asking, "So, what's the worst that could happen? What's the thing you're most scared about doing this deal?" Then, try to encompass some balance to that fear in the agreement so that you're addressing whatever it is they're scared of, and they feel comfortable that that's not going to happen.

The draft agreement is normally a one-page to two- page letter. That's all it takes to get all the clauses and understandings of everything that you're agreeing to in order to do this deal. Once that agreement is done and you've explained every line of it, and they've contributed to it and understand it, you leave it with them.

The problem with most legal agreements is that they suffer from what I call author bias. This means that the person who writes them tends to write them in such a one-sided way that nobody trusts them at all. If you leave the meeting and later send somebody an agreement, they will just assume it has a terrible author bias. They can read completely innocuous clauses as, "This person's trying to take advantage of me." They'll read it as all negative. It's really important that they've collaborated with you, that you've written it together, and you've left it there with them on the day that you've worked together on it. Don't go home and send it to them by email because that kills more deals than almost anything else in this process.

Are We in the Same Ballpark?

Once you've left it with them, you have a period of time when they're still hot, and you can get a deal done. Wait too long, and it gets harder. I went through this dozens of times before I worked it out. Deals are like concrete: the longer you leave them, the harder they get. You need to make sure that you strike while the iron is hot. Otherwise:

- You call in a week: "Yeah, still thinking about it."
- Two weeks later: "Yeah, still haven't had time to think about it."

- Three weeks later, after the fourth call: "Still thinking about it."
- Four weeks, seven calls and finally calling them from another number: "Still thinking."
- Five weeks: No answer
- Six weeks: They've changed their number, name, and left the country.

My advice to Harbour Club members is to wait two to three days, so they've had the time to think about it. You then call them and say, "Have you thought about it?" The answer 99% of the time is, "No. I've been busy. I've been doing this and that, and I haven't had a chance to look at it."

You need to polarize them—make them go in one direction or the other. Find out whether there's a possible deal or if it's a dead duck. Say, "Okay. I understand, you haven't had a chance to think about it yet, but are we roughly on the same page? Or are we in completely different ballparks?"

The answer you're looking for is, "Well, yeah, more or less, but I don't like, X, Y, Z." Or, "More or less, but I don't think I want to give up all the company for a dollar." You're eliciting an extra objection.

If they say, "No, we're not even in the same ballpark," then at least you know it's not the deal for you, and you need to go and kiss a different frog to see if there's a prince or princess inside that one.

Polarize them, so you know if it's worth spending any more time on it.

They've Got a Big But

If they agree that you're on the same page and give you a "but…" (a very important word), then we do a, "No one leaves until…" meeting. Say:

"Okay, how about I come and see you on Friday, at 2 o'clock, and we agree that we'll just sit there and go through this? And none of us are going to leave until we've got the deal in place that works for everyone. If we need to order pizza at midnight, we'll order pizza at midnight. But we'll just sit there and get this thing done."

As soon as they agree to that meeting, they've basically closed. The deal can move a lot in that meeting, and it can change quite considerably from the one that you've fleshed out in the set of terms. They've had more time to think about it, you've had more time to think about it, and the deal that ends up being done in that meeting tends to be the right one.

This meeting creates a time limit around getting an agreement. If you don't create that time limit, the deal can drag on and on. Businesses don't often get themselves out of trouble. They tend to get themselves into more trouble the longer they continue doing the same kind of things.

When I did that first deal with the telecom company, I had the ticking time bomb of the lease expiring and the bulldozers revving up. This strategy replaces the bulldozers. It creates some time pressure when, really, there isn't any. It helps drag the transaction over the line.

 ### Deal Deep Dive: Daniel's Print Company

Daniel, a repeat Harbour Clubber (three times and counting), bought a printing company using the techniques shared in the book. When he sat down and did the initial term sheet, he was going to take an 80% stake in the company and repay a $200,000 director's loan over the coming years. The director's loan was money the owner had put into the company over the years.

Daniel set up a "No one leaves until…" meeting with the owner, with the goal of finalizing the deal. He ended up taking a 40% stake in the printing company, but the owner wrote off the director's loan.

While Daniel walked into the meeting with a deal in mind, the final deal on the table was completely different. He was open-minded and prepared to negotiate to find the best deal. The final deal was the right deal because it worked for both sides. Clearly, the owner initially valued the money he had put in more highly but, when it came down to it, he still believed in the business and so wanted more equity—a great sign for Daniel that he was buying into a business that was worth saving.

Daniel structured the deal using a Harbour Club agreement, which meant he still had control of the company even though he didn't own the mythical 51%. With 40% of the business, Daniel still called the shots.

———————

CHAPTER 8
THE DARK ART OF BUSINESS VALUATION

Never test the depth of the river with both feet.

I call it the dark art of business valuation because there are a lot of charlatans in that world. Business valuation is interesting and massively misunderstood. There are businesses that make money valuing businesses, which I find incredible because the real definition of what a business is worth is what somebody pays for it. In fact, that's all the tax man cares about—how much somebody paid for the shares in the company. That's the true definition of value. Years ago, when I first started out buying and selling businesses, I asked a business broker how he valued a company. He said, "You take the number of directors and multiply it by a million," which was his facetious way of saying everybody wants to take a million off the table, so that's the valuation.

I have heard that Harvard Business School teaches 126 different valuation models. All of those are wrong. There are 126 wrong methodologies for valuing a business because basically, a business is worth what somebody pays for it. Simple.

What is a business valuation, why is it a big industry, and why is Harvard Business School teaching 126 methodologies if they're all wrong? When it comes to valuing a company, you basically make up the number. You pull a number out of thin air and then use one of the 126 Harvard Business School models to justify the number that you have just made up.

Remember doing your mathematic exam at school, where you get one point for the answer and one point for showing your work? If somebody asks, "How much do you want for your business?" and you say, "A million dollars, because I've seen this house for $700,000 and then I'd like to buy a Porsche." That doesn't really work. They don't care what you personally want. But if you say, "I want $1 million because that represents six times price-earnings multiple and I have seen other companies in the same sector selling for about six times price-earnings multiple," they'll say, "Oh, right, okay, that makes sense."

All you've really done is used the valuation metric of a price-earnings multiple to support the number that you just made up. Now price-earnings multiples have loads of different variables. Also, they don't fit that many scenarios. You have to come up with more creative methods of valuing to justify all the various different types of transactions that you might do, for example, when there aren't any earnings.

Here are the four most common valuation methods you'll come across:

> **Return on Net Assets:** Basically, it's talking about the yield that someone will get on their capital. This is often used when you're pitching a property transaction, like a rental property. You might talk about the yield that that person's going to get on their capital (i.e. the "cap rate") as a way of justifying the price

that you're charging. So, instead of the made-up number, you could say, "Because you're going to get a 6% return on capital employed,"—which is a healthy risk-weighted return on capital compared to a benchmark.

Discounted Cash Flow: This is used when justifying assets on balance sheets for companies to an auditor, or any business where you have a contracted revenue stream. A good example is a loan or leasing company, where there are many leases signed up or different customers with associated income streams. Effectively, you sum the total amount that's going to be received over the total term of all the contracts. This gives you one big number, which you then you reduce a little as a risk discount. Let's say you have $5 million of lease payments that are due to come in over the next five years. You might ask for $4 million as the discounted cash-flow way of calculating the valuation. This is a massive oversimplification, but that's the basic idea.

Price-earnings (P/E) ratio: This is probably the most common one because it's one of the key metrics that public companies use (and it's one of the key fields you'll see next to the stocks and shares listings). It's liable to manipulation because you have things like a trailing P/E, which is obviously a multiple of what the company did the previous year. You can also have a forward P/E, which is a multiple of what it will do next year and highly subjective. You can have a P/E-based on an adjusted net profit figure. Brokers are famous for adjusting their net profit, which means it's not its real profit; it's a profit it might have done if they'd done things completely differently, which is obviously dumb but, nonetheless, smart people seem to fall for it.

Barrier to Entry: This final one is quite useful when your business doesn't make any money. I've sold a few of these.

A barrier to entry valuation is what it would cost somebody else to get to a similar position to where you are now. So, for example, you might have a health club and spa in a nice downtown location with one thousand members. What would it cost somebody else to find a decent location, fit it out as a health club and spa, and get up to their first thousand members? It might not make any money at all, but what would it cost somebody else to get there? It might be interesting to a competitor to cut out all the time and money that would otherwise have to be invested.

I remember a deal with a furniture manufacturer on that basis. The furniture manufacturer had patterns, customers, and expertise in a factory that was able to produce those items. What would it cost competitors to get to that point? I used that as the justification for the number that I had made up.

When you're thinking about valuation, it's easy to get lost in everything you read. People who have been reading Mashable or TechCrunch assume that their start-up is worth 100 times their revenue, or some other crazy amount. The kind of strategic acquisition or Silicon Valley acquisition is not the norm. These are perversions in the economy, and you really shouldn't plan your business around getting some insane valuation.

Business Breakout: The Demographic Cliff

There is an issue right now in the SME business world, which is the demographic cliff, where we have many more old people than we do young people. On top of that, these young people want to do something in the block chain space, or they want an app, or they want some tech-based business. They don't want to take over some traditional plumbing and heating business, PR company, or normal business that perhaps their parents would have run.

Two things are colliding: baby boomers are retiring at an astronomical rate (in the US, it's around 11,000 a day) and for the first time in history, the next generation is smaller than the last. In the UK, adult diapers outsell baby diapers. So, with a smaller next generation, there simply aren't the number of people willing or able to take over the retirees' businesses. The impact of this is that valuations (the actual ones, not those made up) for SMEs have plummeted. In the US, it's about one and a half times earnings. Can you believe that? You can have a business that's making a million dollars, and it's selling for one and a half million dollars.

What ends up happening is that people advertise these businesses for sale for a figure they'll never get. After two or three years of not being able to sell, they wind the company down over the next few years, taking as much cash out as possible. They close the doors and walk away. More businesses are being wound down than actually sold. It is not uncommon to find businesses listed on these websites that have been for sale for more than eight years, and, by my unscientific reckoning, only about 10% of the businesses advertised on the major websites actually seem to sell. The net effect of all this for you is that it is a massive buyers' market, but the sellers don't know it yet.

Drivers for the Price-Earnings Ratio

Earnings are the profit from the company, but what changes that multiple in front to give you a P/E ratio? Why are some things three times and some things thirty times? It's all about risk reduction. If there's a lower risk for the buyer, then the multiple tends to increase.

Things that tend to reduce risk are contracted or recurring revenue, which means the businesses that aren't only as good as their last month's sales figures tend to attract a higher multiple because they have recurring income. Of course, you have to look out for contracts that expire in two or three years because they create drop-dead dates in income.

Having multiple products is important. Having high exposure to a single product or a single service can be a risk factor—likewise, single markets and territories, high concentration on a particular customer or within a particular geographic region, all can reduce your overall ability to demand more money for the business. These risk factors will make the buyer want to push the price down.

Then there are scale and liquidity.

The scale paradox is the concept that you have to be big to get big. Once you break beyond a certain size, it's much easier to pitch for bigger contracts, win bigger pieces of business and higher-margin pieces of business. Therefore, scale, which is one of the biggest barriers to getting big, is a risk-reducing factor and drives up valuations.

Once you get above about $100 million in value, there is a massive private equity market that creates some real perversions in valuation. For example, where I live in Singapore, we have numerous private equity companies that have funds specifically for the healthcare sector and with a minimum deal size of $100 million. As soon as a healthcare company comes on the market that's worth more than $100 million, there's a huge bidding war. The last transaction I saw was forty times earnings for a business because the private equity companies are mandated to buy this kind of business.

You get these silly perversions of valuations when companies get on the radar of private equity companies with cash that they have to deploy. In Singapore alone, we have $150 billion of cash sitting waiting to be deployed in private equity. There's plenty of money there if you can fix the scale issue.

The final driver is liquidity. I describe liquidity as a publicly listed company that you can invest in the morning and divest in the afternoon. If you have liquidity, that's a big driver for P/E. If you look at the difference between a large company that's private and a large company that's publicly listed, you'll often find there's about a 30% difference between the valuations. That's called the liquidity discount. When you then compare small private companies to large public ones, the spread is even larger. You can find small companies that have a three-times multiple, and you can find public companies in the same sector with a thirty-times multiple, so by adding scale and liquidity, you can increase the price-earnings multiple tenfold.

If you can work with these various aspects, you can improve your P/E ratio. I'm an M&A person. I love mergers and acquisitions. In fact, my solution to every problem in life is to buy a company. You can solve a lot of issues by buying more businesses. You can become bigger, enter new territories and markets, and develop new products through acquisition. You can create liquidity by publicly listing. Many issues can be solved by using M&A as part of your growth strategy and to get to scale. You don't need to worry too much about getting all the synergies worked out and actually joining the businesses together. Sometimes, just putting them under a common holding company can be enough because a buyer, like a private equity company, will probably see all the synergies as an opportunity. I personally don't. I see it as a massive pain, but quite often, people will see it as a big advantage, so it can work really well when it comes to selling.

So, ultimately, valuations are made up, and the valuation metrics, or the valuation models that people talk about, are just the justification for that made-up number.

Deal Deep Dive: The $1 Deal
that Turned into $3 Million

I once had a PR company that specialized in technology PR. It was based in the UK and had been going for twenty years with some great blue-chip clients and a fantastically loyal team of workers. The business suffered some lean years immediately after the dot-com crash, and as a result, had picked up some debt, and poor cash management had brought it to ruin. I was able to acquire the business for $1 on the basis that in a couple of weeks, it would be closed down, a classic hospital pass.

However, with some quick reprioritization and cash management, we were able to rescue the business, and some months later, we were looking for a sale. The business didn't have any tangible assets, but it had a twenty-year reputation and $1 million of revenue that was profitable, if only recently.

We ended up with two possible buyers. One was a UK-based investor willing to pay $231,000, and one was a San Francisco-based tech company looking for a UK office, and that valued it at $3.1 million!

The logic from the US-based company was that they were valued at ten times their annual revenue, so by adding this company, they would increase their valuation by over $10 million. If they could buy the business for $3 million, they would get a valuation arbitrage, which would increase shareholder value.

I found it incredible that they did not look at the business through a lens of "How much is it worth?" This deal was the genesis of my understanding valuations.

From this deal, I also learned that the buying structure is more important than the price. If you can make the purchase affordable from the cash flow of the business, you engage what I call the "buy-to-let mentality." People investing in property focus on the positive carry between the rental income and the mortgage, so they look for the tenant to pay their mortgage and don't worry about the price so much. This is dangerous thinking (interest rate history is one reason!) but is quite common. It can also really work in your favor when selling because you can add a deferred element to the deal that is easily affordable, but really bumps up the overall value.

———————

CHAPTER 9
ALWAYS USE A SPECIAL PURPOSE VEHICLE

*If you know the tightrope is only a few
inches off the ground, how fast do you run?*

Bill Gates was once asked what he thought was the most significant invention in business in the last hundred years. Everyone expected him to say the desktop PC or the internet or something related to his world and career. He said the limited liability company. He felt that the limited liability company was the biggest step forward in the business world in the last hundred years. Why? Because it gave protection of capital for people to invest and take risks. Before the limited liability company, if an investment didn't work out, you lost everything. And if you lost everything you went to jail, at the time they still had debtors' prisons, literally.

After the implementation of the limited liability company, which then made it possible for people to take ring-fenced, isolated risks, there's been a huge boom in economic activity. This has probably done more to improve global living standards than anything else in history.

Business Breakout: Personal Guarantees

I think it's a shame that banks and financial institutions are trying to erode the sanctity of limited liability by imposing personal guarantees. They only target the SME owner, yet SME businesses make up 50% of GDP in most mature economies; they're the life blood of the economy and they employ pretty much all of the private sector workers. Why are they the red-headed stepchild when it comes to taxation, legislation, and banking? This is another example of how, in a large company, the directors aren't obliged to sign any kind of personal guarantee for debt, but if you're a small company and you want to borrow money from a bank, you have to bet your house. It's simply not fair.

There is huge power in the use of a limited liability company. The companies we're acquiring are limited liability companies, and we will always acquire them by using another limited liability company, which is what we call a special purpose vehicle (SPV).

When I talk about buying a company for $1, what actually happens is an SPV buys the shares in the target company for $1.

What is an SPV?

An SPV is simply a registered limited liability company sitting waiting to do a deal. Just a normal run-of-the-mill limited liability company, nothing different or special about it. You can give it any name, any number of directors or shareholders—it doesn't matter, but it's always easier with one director and shareholder when it comes to filling out paperwork. Generally speaking, the SPV should be registered in the country where you are doing the deal.

You can register companies quickly and cheaply, so simply have one set up, ready-to-go, just waiting to do a transaction. The key component of an LLC is its limited liability. Rather than personally buying the company and risking yourself as a contracting party being held liable for something in the future, just putting an SPV in between creates a little more security. The contracting party (the one that enters into the agreements and therefore can be sued for any breach) is a company, not you.

If you have an existing business and you are looking to acquire, you should still use an SPV. Create one that can be standalone or a subsidiary of your current business. Use it to do the deal. Accountants sometimes advise against this because you have to consolidate the accounts, making a little extra accounting work, but it is vitally important that the deal you do uses an empty limited company. As the contracting party, if you buy directly, you open yourself up to litigation risk, and when dealing with distressed businesses, this is a higher than usual risk. Use an SPV, and it is largely mitigated.

YouTube managed to have a huge amount of illegal content for years without ever being sued. As soon as Google bought them, MGM, Fox, and others, whose material had been published illegally, issued a multi-billion-dollar lawsuit, knowing that YouTube could now afford it! I also dealt with a telecom company that bought a customer of theirs (another telco) and spent nearly $500,000 on due diligence. As soon as the deal was closed, they were sued by a staff member who had left six months before they had even started looking to buy the company. The staff member hadn't bothered suing before because he didn't believe the company had the money to pay out, but now it did!

It's important not to throw a rotten apple into your nice clean barrel of shiny ones.

Deal Deep Dive: Building an Empire

When I first started doing deals, I went through what I call my "empire-building phase." I just wanted to buy everything and build it into this giant holding company. I had the holding company at the top, and I just kept adding more and more companies underneath. It created a very pretty organizational structure.

A few things happen when you build an empire:

- You are treated as a group for taxation, and in some countries, taxes are higher for larger companies. None of my businesses were individually large companies, but my group now paid the higher rate of tax.
- Some of the businesses were so small they would not have met the sales tax threshold! However, as a group, you have to register for sales tax for all group companies.
- As a large company, you are required to have a full audit. Small companies are generally exempt. A full audit can be a huge cost, not just to the external provider, but also in terms of internal resources.

While a group structure looks pretty and feels right, it is really an ego thing. You don't need a group: you can just as easily have silos—separate companies that can inter-trade, share resources and office space, and garner all the benefits of a group without the penalties.

So, if you are building an empire, ask yourself if there's a good reason. Don't get me wrong—there are good reasons (e.g., if you want to go public or pitch for bigger contracts), but make sure you have a good reason before you empire-build.

———————

CHAPTER 10
THE DEAL PIE

*When doing deals, structure can
be more important than price.*

Most people think a deal is about how much cash you need now and how much later, and these are the only parameters they consider. It's probably because we are used to buying property, and most people know how to buy a house: cash plus mortgage. That's it.

However, business deals have many more parameters around how you do the cash now and the cash later. When someone says they want a million dollars for their business, don't be dismissive; instead, say, "Okay, let's see how we get you to your million dollars."

This is a powerful sentence: you are not owning the million dollars (that is theirs), but you are offering a collaborative approach to reaching a solution they want. This is the way to do deals with owner-managers and entrepreneurs. Collaborate, don't compete; keep ego intact and work together; put your chair on their side of the desk.

The "Deal Pie"

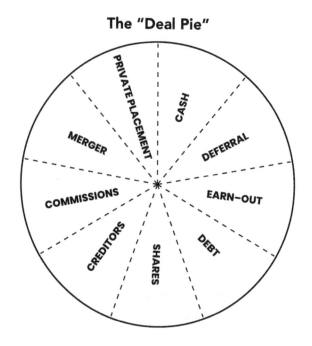

You can then work towards their $1 million with a number of items. We call it a "deal pie," like a pie chart with the components of the $1 million broken out. You can have:

- Cash—this can include cash extracted from the business at purchase and given to the existing shareholders
- Deferral—this is money paid over time
- Earn-out—this is linked to some future performance or success
- Debt—this is like a mortgage borrowed against the business (Many M&A courses teach you to use working capital finance like factoring or invoice finance… do not! It is dangerous, lazy, and simple, and a real wealth hazard—there are much smarter ways to do it.)
- Shares—you can pay the old owners with a share in the company (I explain more in Harbour Club courses), or you can use shares

in a holding company as payment in a roll-up (see more on roll-ups in Chapter 13)

- Creditors—you can do debt-for-equity swaps or get creditors to support the purchase
- Commissions—you can switch suppliers and get kickbacks for long-term contracts
- Merger—you can buy a distressed company for
- $1 and merge this into a target company, which gives you an equity foot in the door
- Private placement—you can get an investor to support a cash component if you have the rest of the deal agreed (but this should only be for large solvent businesses)

In the Harbour Club course, we go through twelve different deal structures (at the time of this writing), showing how you can buy businesses without using cash up front. These are designed to cope with everything from the well-established, profitable, debt-free business right down to the completely distressed basket case that's about to close its doors and send everybody home. We cover the whole spectrum of motivating opportunities. The deal pie sits somewhere in the middle. It's a way of structuring a deal so that you can acquire a decent business. I wouldn't call it a great business, but it is a good business that's probably generating profits, has some assets, and offers a good opportunity to build something for the future.

Business Breakout: The Leveraged Buy-Out Trap

An LBO is far and away the most common no-money-down acquisition strategy that is being taught. It's simple, anybody can do it and it's commonly understood. People are used to the idea of real estate investing, and real estate is a kind of an LBO, because you always have a mortgage and a cash component—they are the only two moving parts. It's an easier hurdle for people to get over if they think of a business deal as a real estate deal. But the beauty about business is there's an infinite number of moving parts—there are so many different facets to a business versus a property. The only limit really is your imagination.

You need to be careful with LBOs. They can be great, but the two most common issues are:

1. Using working capital finance (like invoice finance) so now you have no future cash flow and you get in a real pickle
2. Personal guarantees, where you take on massive amounts of debt and you bet your house, so now you are really tied to working in that business until the full value of the loan is extinguished, or you can literally lose everything

There has to be a time in the entrepreneurial journey when you stop sticking everything on red and spinning the wheel. You only need a financial crisis or interest rate spike to wipe you out. *Be careful.*

When I bought the small IT company mentioned earlier for $1, I ended up merging it with a larger IT company for a 35% stake in the new enlarged business. I then used a combination of shares, earn-out, and deferral to take my stake up 87.5%. The small acquisition effectively became the currency for a bigger deal.

In that situation, it was about using a structure instead of just focusing on the price. How much do you want for your company, and how do we structure this? You don't have to just think in terms of how much money they want, how much of that needs to be up front, and how much you need to borrow from the bank!

When you're buying a company, there's so much more to play with. You've got the shares in the company—you can keep them as a shareholder, you don't have to buy it all. You could buy just 80%. You need to have good contracts in place if you have another shareholder because you need to be able to control the profits, the sale of the business, and a few other things that we cover in the Harbour Club course. Lawyers love huge shareholder agreements, but you can cover all the important things in a couple of pages.

You can use deferral, paying money over time. You can use earn-out. So, don't think of deals in one or two dimensions—think about how to solve the problem with a multifaceted approach.

Choose Your Slices of Pie

There are a lot of different parts to the deal pie, but you don't have to use all of them, because it can get overcomplicated. Just use the ones necessary to get the deal closed.

Earn-out is useful for any excess valuation. If people come up with a crazy number, ask them why they think it's worth that ridiculous number, and they'll give you some jam tomorrow story about how great next year's going to be. Let's face it, all entrepreneurs think their best year ever is going to be next year. You can say, "Well, if you achieve all those things, then we will give you this extra money." You're saying, "Look, if you make me $10 million, I'll give you $2 million." So, when people over-value their business or assume some amazing future performance, you can build this into the earn-out, as earn-out is a payment linked to a specific performance; in effect, you are making it self-funding.

You can give a little cash by borrowing some money against the business and giving it to them.

Some caveats: first, be careful with term loans that don't have any personal guarantees. Getting such loans is difficult, though, because not many banks will do deals without personal guarantees.

Second, also avoid leveraging the debtors. Don't use invoice financing. It's common and very tempting because you can see the accounts receivable ledger and the invoice finance company will give you 80% of that in cash, so it looks like a quick way of getting a chunk of cash to give to the previous owner. But the problem is that when you take that cash and give it to the previous owner, effectively what you've done is taken the working capital out of the business and given it to somebody who's run off into the sunset. You'll have a huge pinch on your cash flow in the months (up to a year) ahead, which will be hard to survive. The factoring or invoice finance companies make good fees from you while you're trading, but as soon as you go into default, they make massive fees. The first wobble and they stick the knife in.

I'm not a big fan of the leverage approach, but deferral is a great example of shifting the burden to the previous owner, like vendor finance. Pitch the idea of deferral:

> "Hey, look before the banking crisis of 2008, it was dead easy to get the bank to finance these kinds of transactions, but now the banks don't finance this—you're going to have to. I'm going to pay you a chunk of money over a period of time instead of getting the bank loan that I perhaps might have done in the past."

That's a reasonably plausible way to position yourself for a deferred payment type structure.

Money Up Front?

What if they insist on having some money up front? Then maybe it's not the deal to do. If they insist on money up front, I always say,

"Look, if you've got somebody who's willing to give you this money now up front, take it, go for it. If you haven't, here's my deal. Here's the deal that we've got on the table." You'd be surprised how many times, when you stick it out, you can actually get the deal done for no money up front. You're a path of least resistance, you're a simple person to do a deal with, and there are very few simple people to do a deal with out there. By focusing on the structure instead of the price, you can often get deals done that no one else can and then swoop in and run off with all the prizes.

Deal Deep Dive: Steve and the Elderly Owner

Steve came along to the Harbour Club in August 2017. By Friday, August 11, just a few days later, he had his first lead, a company insurance inquiry that came into his independent financial advice (IFA) firm.

Steve noticed that the company owner was seventy-two, that the company had a strong balance sheet, and made an average profit of $200,000 per year. The elderly owner wanted to retire and spend time with his second wife, who was twenty-seven years younger than he was. He hadn't spent much time with his first wife because he was running the business, and after she died, he realized the importance of family time. He had no other offers on the table, although his accountant had been trying to sell the company for him. Steve was considered an experienced person to be trusted to safeguard his legacy and his staff.

Steve got on well with the owner. They respected each other. Steve commented, "We could have got a deal done over a glass of wine and drafted our own contracts."

That would have been the right way to do it. As soon as the lawyers got involved, the whole thing slowed down and almost died.

The business highlights were:

- a long-established niche market with good repeat business
- $200,000 annual profit
- cash in the bank
- a debt-free property worth $1 million that was part subleased to another company providing a nice additional income stream
- no debt

The company occupied a small industrial site in the Midlands, UK. The whole site was his factory plus another part of the industrial site that was sublet to somebody else. The total official evaluation came up with around £1 million for the real estate. Real estate in the Midlands in England is relatively inexpensive, hence the smaller evaluation.

As we mentioned at the beginning of the chapter, Steve presented various strategies from the "deal pie" to the owner with a pretty healthy £1.7 million headline number. However, none of it came from Steve. While the seller felt this was a great solution to getting him out and free (the real motivation), there were two roadblocks to the deal. First, the accountant claimed that, "If Steve is not putting any cash in, we can get a better deal." Steve pointed out the accountant had been trying to sell it already and had not been able to, so why would he suddenly be able to do better? The second roadblock was the family for the same reason. There was only one shareholder, but there seemed to be multiple decision-makers, or at least influencers, so Steve had to then build rapport with the family as well to show he was to be trusted. He invited the family to his home, and that personal meeting clinched the deal.

The deal amounted to £1.7 million, made up of a £450,000 initial payment (paid from the company's own money) and the balance deferred at £200,000 a year for six years. Steve didn't have to part with any of his own cash. He learned a lot from the negotiation, especially noting how crucial the head of terms (or letter of intent) meeting was, because, without it, the deal would have fallen apart.

Being patient is a virtue, because doing a deal can be a bumpy road at times. Steve says, "Avoid lawyers if you can; if not, make sure both sides are on a fixed fee. I would even go as far as to pay for both sides' legal fees if it gets the deal done quicker." Steve's lawyer worked on a fixed fee totaling £8,844; the other side spent £39,860 on lawyers' fees. The legal team for the seller was not on a fixed fee, so they were motivated to drag the deal out and earn a small fortune in the process.

The LOI meeting was referred back to multiple times.

Deal Fatigue

The seller's lawyers did a great job of dragging the deal out. Part of the legal noise that cropped up was the fact that Steve was going to be paying the seller money over the next five years. Steve was taking on a bank loan and taking some money out of the business' bank account. The seller's lawyer was worried that, if Steve didn't pay the bank loan, then the bank would pull the rug out from underneath them and take all the real estate away, leaving no security for the five years' worth of deferred payments.

Steve's solution was simply to extend the payout period. So, instead of it being five years, he stretched it out to seven years. If Steve had made that offer originally, he probably wouldn't have got as far as the LOI meeting and possibly not even as far as having a handshake on the deal. But, at the eleventh hour, deal fatigue had set in. Everybody was at the point of giving up and beginning to think, "Whatever it takes, let's just get this thing over the line."

Originally, Steve wanted to use a traditional lender for a property loan to release cash into the deal, but they were horrendous to deal with, so he quickly dropped them in favor of a longer, deferred payment plan.

This also meant leaving the assets unencumbered (no mortgage), which made the seller more comfortable and, with no bank in the deal, there were fewer fees and less legal involvement. He plans to avoid property lending at the beginning of a deal in the future, maybe introducing it as part of a deferred payment or a refinance once in control.

Of course, costs were incurred, including legal fees, survey fees, and taxes totaling $18,538, with $1,194 not reclaimed as an expense item.

Steve implemented the Harbour Club turnaround strategies. The business was not distressed, but obviously, if you apply these strategies to a good business, they make it even better. He took the $200,000 annual profit to a run rate of $350,000 per year and was able to extract some previously unexploited research and development tax claims, with over $30,000 already received and a further $150,000 in process—some nice quick wins.

Based on his success, Steve is now actively looking to bolt on another company in the industrial or engineering sector to get a bit more scale, and then possibly look at agglomeration in the sector because it is highly fragmented; there are many small players without much idea around succession. It would be ideally suited for a collaborative roll-up strategy.

Steve owns an IFA firm, and through its clients, he has sourced two good deals so far.

Using another tactic Steve learned in the Harbour Club course, he has accelerated the process of selling the IFA business and will now get quite a significant price premium, giving him another extra $1 million from the deal versus a normal exit. Steve said, "I am adding a minimum extra $1 million to my net worth from the deal. It still blows my mind that within a year of doing the Harbour Club course, I am going to make an extra $1 million!"

Business Breakout: Tax Issues

In the UK, we have entrepreneur's relief. Of course, taxes are different for everybody, but for people based in the UK, they can get entrepreneur's relief and only pay 10% tax. It's more tax-efficient for the government to give them their own money than it is for them to take their own money. As crazy as it sounds, it is true in a lot of different legal jurisdictions around the world. Get tax-savvy!

Business Breakout: Spotting the Signs

Do you have deals in your current company? Your customers? Your suppliers? Is your next deal in your phone? Your next deal might be in one of the conversations that you're already having. You just haven't looked at it through that particular lens before or tuned into what people are really saying. Stop thinking about what you're going to say, listen to what the other person is saying, and look for the signs that pop up in everyday conversation.

CHAPTER 11
MERGERS

If you can't buy them, join them.

W e've looked at how you might structure a deal with a deal pie, so now let's have a look at mergers.

Learning by Teaching

Sitting down and working out exactly how I made deals was an eye-opener. You only really understand the topic when you have to teach it to someone, because you have to granularize it and break it down into its core components, then put it back together to explain it to someone.

When I started the Harbour Club back in 2009, I was buying and selling companies, but I wasn't paying close attention to what I was doing. Finding deals was the thing I was always asked about, not necessarily the process that followed.

Right at the beginning of creating the course, I did what a lot of people do and googled, "how to buy a business no money down," and other variations. At that time, there weren't any training courses on how to buy businesses, apart from maybe MBA ones, and there was nothing on no-money-down transactions beyond the typical LBO type of solution. Even those were few and far between in terms of their promotion. There were forums with articles saying that you can't buy businesses without any money, which is a common fallacy. Forums tend to be operated by brokers as a way of generating leads, so of course, brokers don't want to perpetuate the idea that you can do no-money-down deals because that means they don't receive a commission. A post on one of the forums said the only way you're going to find a deal that doesn't require any money up front is if it is so insolvent that it's pretty much going to fail and leave you with all the liabilities of the company.

The other scaremongering I found on the forum was that people would need to borrow so much money that the business would fall over under the weight of its own debt.

I popped on to this forum, and I asked, "What about a merger?"

Business Breakout: Stupid Business Advice is Everywhere

How stupid does business advice have to be to misrepresent the basic principle of limited liability? Limited liability companies are the eighth wonder of the world and, unless you operate them fraudulently, basically the debts of the company belong to the company, not the owners of the company. If you were a shareholder in Enron, Bear Stearns, Lehmann Brothers or World Com, you had a pretty torrid time from an investment standpoint; your $100 worth of shares may have ended up worthless, but nobody came after you for the billions of dollars that were lost to everybody else. So, it is absolutely stupid, ridiculous, nonsense to suggest that, if you buy an insolvent company and it fails, you're suddenly liable for all those debts. Read the chapter on always using an SPV.

This toxic idea permeates business advice. People are worried about their credit rating if they're a director of a company or a shareholder in a company that becomes bankrupt. Through necessity, not choice, as company director, I have personally pulled more than a dozen companies through insolvency. It's the fiduciary duty of the director to appoint a bankruptcy attorney if the business is unable to meet its debts and they fall due. It's the legally correct thing to do. I've also been involved in many other companies where this has been the outcome that's had to be dealt with. And I don't have any problems with credit rating.

What About a Merger?

A merger is an acquisition of a company using shares instead of cash. Instead of paying cash to complete the contract, you give up equity in your business.

It's absolutely a no-money-down transaction. You give up equity in your business and gain another business.

Why would you do a merger if all that happens is you double in size, but you end up with half the company? Isn't that standing still? Well, no, and I'll give you a few killer reasons why you should look at doing a merger.

Reason 1: Synergies

This reason isn't my favorite, but it seems to be everyone else's favorite. Synergies are the opportunities for cross-selling things that are duplicated between the two companies. So effectively you might have two offices, two accounting departments, two of everything, and maybe you only need one of everything, or one and a half of everything. Synergies can add money straight to the bottom line, and money straight to the bottom line goes straight to your valuation because most companies' value is justified by a multiple of their profits. This has a positive impact on the overall shareholder value.

The other potential option is what's called an "accretive merger." This is where your valuation is greater than the multiple that you offer in terms of your shares.

"Accretive" is the opposite of "dilutive." *Dilutive* means that there are more shares in issue sharing the same profit, therefore the earnings per share goes down. *Accretive* means that there are more shares in issue, but there's more profit per share, so the earnings per share goes up. And if earnings per share go up, then the fundamental value goes up, and the company is worth more per share, and worth more in total.

This is common with larger companies acquiring smaller companies with their shares, because larger companies are valued at a higher multiple of earnings, and smaller companies have fewer options open to them, so they will accept lower valuations in terms of shares. You effectively get an accretive impact.

An accretive merger can also be a powerful way to create shareholder value.

Reason 2: Best Practice

Best practice is looking at two similar companies and seeing how they arrive at their results. Company X and Company Y could have $1 million gross annual revenue with $100,000 profit, but how they get from their $1 million top line to their $100,000 bottom line might be very different. Some companies might be operationally strong, while others might be strong on sales and marketing. Best practice is about finding the best versions between those two. Using the great sales and marketing of one coupled with the great operational delivery of the other means that you can get this "two plus two equals six" effect when you put the two companies together.

Reason 3: Quick Scale with No Cash

This is where it gets really interesting. You get a quick scale with no cash. In business, big is beautiful. When you become bigger, you get on the radar of many more potential buyers, and it is easier to win bigger contracts and grow. So, by making your business bigger, you're immediately more attractive. In fact, if you go over the $5 million revenue mark, you tend to arrive on the radar of a number of acquirers within your trade just because at that level, it's worth their spending the money on the due diligence to buy you, as you're going to have a meaningful impact on the growth of their business.

Reason 4: Succession Planning

One of the best uses of the merger structure is for succession planning. It really is, and here's why. Succession planning is a massive pain because the problem with selling a business is that you effectively have to sell yourself with the business. You are one of the operationally important people in the business and will end up being tied to it by some kind of earn-out golden handcuffs, consultancy agreement, whatever.

A great example I can share is about one of the Harbour Clubbers who came to us a few years ago. We'll call him Bob. After doing the Harbour Club course, Bob did a merger rather than take our advice and do succession planning first. Like many business owners, he looked at the upside of a merger, which was that he would continue to earn revenue by working in the business. In succession planning, he would earn profit as a shareholder rather than working in the business.

Looking only at the upside, Bob decided that he wanted to be the chief executive officer (CEO) of the new entity formed as a result of the merger. The other owner, we'll call him Ted, became a passive 50%

shareholder and founder of the new business he formed with Bob. For the next ten years, Bob worked in the business while Ted sat around and did nothing. At this time, a well-known private equity company offered the entity $18 million. The offer was a great deal if your name was Ted because terms dictated that $9 million came in the form of cash to the founder and $9 million came in the form of shares. Bob was the CEO, not the founder or the shareholder. Bob was the guy saddled with delivering everything on the business. This is a perfect example as to how the guy in charge effectively gets screwed when a merger is not structured correctly.

It's always best to have your succession plan in place well before you're going to sell the business. You want to sell it with a management team in place, and you want to be a shareholder, not an owner/manager and not an owner/operator.

Now, the problem with succession planning is that you have to go out and recruit somebody to take your place and recruiting somebody can be a minefield; after all, they may or may not be good at the job. You don't want someone too entrepreneurial; you want someone who will just sail the ship. But the problem with employees is they're never as devoted to the company as an owner/manager.

It's hard to find somebody to replace a good entrepreneurial CEO. In fact, sometimes, it takes two or three people to deliver the same result as one entrepreneurial CEO.

You also tend to damage your profitability by hiring someone to replace you because entrepreneurial CEOs who own the business tend to do it as much for the love and the passion they have for the business as they do for the monetary side. They tend to be massively underpaid for the value that they're delivering. As soon as you have to pay somebody of the same caliber to do the same thing, it will have an impact on the overall profitability of the business and therefore make the business worth a little bit less when it comes to selling it.

Now, if you want to find somebody who's good at running a business that looks like yours, they're probably running a business that looks like yours right now. So, in essence, you want to find a management team in a business that looks like yours and merge with them. As part of that merger, you take on their management team. And the great thing is, they'll want the job.

Synergies Suck

Here's why I don't like the synergies option: if you focus on delivering all those synergies, in my experience, what tends to happen is the business goes down a little in the short term. You might get some benefits from those synergies over a two- to three-year time horizon, but in the short term, you tend to disrupt the business quite a bit. It might seem obvious that if you fire Deirdre the bookkeeper, you save $30,000 a year, and your business is now "worth more" in total value. But what actually happens when you get rid of Deirdre the bookkeeper is you spend the next six months arguing with the management team about why you fired Deirdre the bookkeeper. All their focus is on Deirdre the bookkeeper, not where it should be.

I prefer to sell the dream, not the actuality. So, put the two businesses under a common holding company and then offer it for sale with the possibility of all these synergies for the next guy. People always look at synergies as being really simple to execute, but they're actually a real pain and require an awful lot of management time. I prefer to spend my time as a shareholder rather than as an on-the-ground operator. If you do create a reasonable amount of shareholder value right away through the merger of the two entities, messing around with the synergies bit is only a small incremental percentage of growth in the merged entity. The opportunity cost of getting lost down that rabbit hole, and the potential to mess things up as much as you make things better, means the juice isn't worth the squeeze at the end of the day.

How to Double Your Business Tomorrow

You can find a merger partner, put the two companies together and be twice the size. You do this with a newly created SPV—the company that you use to do the transaction. This effectively becomes the holding company for the two companies that you want to merge.

Then each of the two companies simply swap their shares into the holding company and the holding company's capital table, or its share register, becomes the mixture of the shareholders from the two entities that you're merging. The percentage that you merge them at is, of course, entirely up to you; you can merge based on any valuation or metric that you choose.

I once approached the merger conversation by asking someone how much their business was worth. He said $1 million, which is a common answer to that question. I asked him how he came up with a million dollars. His reasoning was, "We're making $100,000 a year of profit, so ten times $100,000 is a million."

I said, "Brilliant, I'm making $50,000 a year of profit, so ten times $50,000 is $500,000, so I'll have a third and you have two thirds." He couldn't argue with his own logic. He came up with the valuation model, and it actually happened to suit me particularly well because we were much, much smaller than he was, and so I was happy to take his metric.

You can value a business by gross annual revenue, number of subscribers, gross profit, net profit, or net asset value on the balance sheet. Pretty much whatever metric you choose, you can use as a valuation method. When you look at two businesses side by side, you're going to choose the one that's probably the most advantageous for you and come up with some arguments as to why that's the best methodology to use to merge the businesses.

There are no rules. The wonderful thing about business is that you can be as creative as you like in how you structure these deals. It's easy to come up with a million different ways to make it really interesting.

Deal Deep Dive: Taking an 87.5% Stake

After we bought an IT company, we then found a bigger IT company down the road that was doing about £1.2 million in revenue at the time, and we agreed to do a merger whereby we would get about a 30% stake in the IT company for merging their business with this little IT company that we had acquired for nothing. In effect, we would get rid of the cost base, put all our customers in there, and end up with a 30% stake in the new enlarged business. We then agreed to give the CEO, the guy from the bigger business, quite a bit of money taken from the profits of the company over time, to take our stake up to 87.5%.

We did that through two different mechanisms:

- A deferral—a fixed amount of money that we paid over a fixed period of time, effectively waiving our dividend rights for a period of time and him taking all the cash out.
- An earn-out—whereby we gave him a share of the sales generated from the extra upside created by the crossover between the two businesses (the combination of the deferral and the earn-out over the next eighteen months to two years took us up to an 87.5% stake in the business)

CHAPTER 12
BUY IN, BUY OUT

Business is all about having more money coming in than going out.

The "Buy In, Buy Out" (BIBO) strategy is where we use our cash flow and financial engineering tactics to take a sweat equity stake in a business, and then sell it back to the founder once it is fixed. They pay you out of the future profits (see below).

You might find a business that has cash flow problems. They are looking for you to invest $100,000 for 30%. You show them how you can fix their problems without the need for $100,000 and make the business more cash-flow positive in the future. Is that worth 30% still? Of course. So, then you have 30% of a profitable and cash-positive business. The one person in the world who will value this share above everyone else is the founder/owner. Your work is done: you have added the real value for your share, so why don't they buy you out?

You can be totally upfront about this, explaining that as soon as it is fixed, you would like an exit, whether that is to sell the whole business or for them to buy you out. It is important to have a well-worded contract to support this. The Harbour Club contract is just two pages.

I discovered the BIBO completely by accident. It was actually something that went wrong that led to me doing a BIBO, and since then, it's been a useful tactic. I took a 50% stake in a business process outsourcer. I had fixed the fundamental issues, but after time had struggled to add more value. We got a few new clients but also lost a few, so the business was really standing still. I was able to sell my stake back to management and exit that way.

When I explained this at the Harbour Club, people saw it as a great way to replace their income so that they could engage with the Harbour Club full time. It, therefore, became a part of the course. This is probably the path of least resistance transaction because it's the easiest transaction compared with all the different structures. If you don't already have a business and you're not acquiring a competitor or merging with somebody else, this is probably the easiest standalone buy/sell deal that you can do.

To make it work, we use several financial engineering techniques that we've worked out over the years. Typically, these can return between 10% and 15% of the company's gross annual revenue back to the business in cash. Obviously, that has a huge impact on the profitability and cash flow for the business.

Essentially, a BIBO deal asks how much that result is worth to the business owner. If you can make a big increase in their profit, gross annual revenue, and cash flow, how much is that worth to them? You then put that in an equity term. Harbour Clubbers have taken between 20% and 80% stakes in businesses in exchange for fixing something—for adding value to the business.

If you think about it, if a business is breaking even, or losing a little bit of money every year, and you suddenly parachute 10% or 15% of its gross annual revenue back into that business in cash or profit, you've basically added huge amounts of value. You might have a business that was about to close its doors or was really struggling to make ends meet and, all of a sudden, you've got a business that's generating high amounts of cash on a month-on-month basis. How much is that worth to the founder?

Even without learning these techniques, it is still relatively easy to get a stake in a small company by investing your time, fixing a problem, or adding value. Identify the issue and pitch your solution.

A 51% Share is a Myth

You take a stake in the business in exchange for fixing a problem. The most important thing is that you don't then end up as a passenger, because you don't want to be a 20%, 30%, 40% shareholder in a business where you don't have any control, the other guy just does whatever they want, and you're just along for the ride whether you like it or not.

Through hard lessons at the Harbour Club, we've learned not to use a lawyer to draft a shareholder's agreement because this can sometimes cost tens of thousands of dollars. Instead, we use five simple clauses that will give you complete control of the business, enable you to buy the company, sell the company, and take profits out. You can do all the things that you need to do while only being a minority shareholder.

Forget the 51% thing. It's a bit of a myth anyway. You just need the right clauses in your agreement, and then you can pretty much do what you'd like with the business. None of the clauses we use in all our Harbour Club agreements suffer from author bias. We have win-win contract terms, not author-biased contract terms.

So, go in, take a stake in a business, fix the problems, then create a company loan to effectively sell that stake straight back to the owner. If you think about it, the worst thing in their life is this business issue. You go in and fix that issue for them, and then they fall in love with their business again. They're the prime candidate to buy the company.

So, how can they afford to buy the company back from you? It comes back to deferral: they can pay you from the profits of the company. However, when you are selling a company, you have to be careful with deferral, because you might not get the money.

How to Make Deferred Payments Work

When it comes to selling a business, or a share in a business, like in a BIBO, it is common to have a portion up front and a portion deferred (i.e., paid later). Deferral is not the same as earn-out. Earn-out is linked to a specific performance—you have to achieve something to get it, like a profit target or customer retention. Deferral is a fixed amount of money over a period of time. You will often hear people say, "Be happy with the upfront payment because you won't ever get the deferral," and unfortunately, that's often true. The deferred element becomes a resented payment each month, and eventually, people begin to talk themselves into not paying it. You end up fighting it legally with their defense based on implied warranty, "He told me it was black; it is actually a very dark blue." Also, the legal system is so unfair that it can cost you many tens of thousands of dollars just to get to bring the matter to court, and then you are relying on the mood of the judge for a positive outcome. If you wanted to get security like a debenture or a personal guarantee, the seller's accountant or lawyer would simply dismiss it out of hand, particularly when you are selling a small stake in the business.

However, if the buyer were to take out a loan, it would be perfectly normal to ask for a debenture (a full fixed and floating charge over the assets of the company). It's also normal for the lender to charge interest and an arrangement fee, all things that you would not expect to get approved in a deferral agreement.

The answer is to use your own loan company, one that you create for this purpose. Now you are able to say, "I will sell you my 30% for $150,000, and I have a company that will give you the loan to do so." The buyer then enters into a loan agreement and debenture with the loan company for $150,000, and you hand over your shares. As they make repayments to the loan company, the loan company sends you the money. The loan company does not physically have to have the money; it simply processes the payments. In the event that they stop paying, you can foreclose on the whole business (not just the 30%), and the legal case is black and white: "We lent you money, pay us our money." They can't wriggle and argue and moralize on that one!

There are so many uses for this structure that we have found through the Harbour Club that it is a great way to deal with large payments. If you are providing a loan for a business in most countries, it is totally unregulated. All the regulation is around consumer loans.

This next deep dive is a good example of how to use deferred payments as a constructive solution.

Deal Deep Dive: How Much is It Worth to Somebody?

My first BIBO was an IT company based in Hampshire, UK that was doing about £1.2 million a year. It was about ten years old when I came across it, and I helped it make a good bit of money and gave the owner the opportunity to take some cash out of the business. In exchange, I took an 87.5% stake in it. Essentially, I picked up for a pound a distressed IT company that was invoicing about half a million a year, and I just moved all those IT contracts into this newly expanded company.

Instantly, I grew the business by about 40% from a top-line perspective. Then, from the bottom line, the extra cash production that was being generated allowed the owner to take money out of the business over a period of time, so he effectively ended up with 12.5%, and I ended up with 87.5%.

My plan was to go and do that again and again and effectively go and find many other distressed IT companies (or even perfectly solvent IT companies), merge them together and create one big IT company. But I was still pretty young and green at the time so, while it was a great idea, it wasn't one that was met with the greatest of abilities. I pitched lots of different IT companies, trying to put a deal together, but couldn't quite get any of them to close. I had a few near misses but didn't manage to drag any over the finish line.

Of course, if I were doing it today, I wouldn't find it difficult at all. But back then, it was just a little bit too early in my career to pull the transactions off. So after about a year and a half of not being terribly successful and, of course, the one who had the 12.5% was relying on my ability to be able to do just that, I decided that the opportunity cost of carrying on with that strategy was too great and that I needed to move on to doing more deals that were easy—actually buying and selling companies.

So, I figured I would look at how we could do a management buy-out, effectively getting the management team to buy you out. Now, of course, the management team, in this case, was the previous owner of the business, and he didn't have that much money. He had used the money I had allowed him to take off the table to resolve certain personal debt issues and give himself some breathing space after being an entrepreneur for twenty years, which we all know can be financially damaging. It wasn't a "retirement sum" that he'd been given.

However, he was still the obvious buyer because people who run a business, or entrepreneurs who have founded a business, always see more value in their own business than anybody else does. It's a blessing and a curse, this entrepreneurial optimism. I realized that he was the perfect buyer, so I used our loan company structure to finance the deal so that the purchaser could pay us over time. I created a five-year loan for the previous owner to buy me out. It was an elegant solution.

It took nearly two years to complete this transaction from start to finish. I realized that, if you focus on the end result when you start a deal, it will get done more quickly—in fact, Harbour Clubbers have now been doing such deals with two- to three-month turnaround times.

CHAPTER 13
VIRTUAL MERGER 2.0—AGGLOMERATION

The Scale Paradox is that you have to be big to get big.

Look where all the money in the world is:

- $30 trillion is in equities ($30,000,000,000,000)—that is a tiny fraction of a small percentage of companies (the ones that lobby governments and employ a tiny number of people in percentage terms)
- $70 trillion is debt ($70,000,000,000,000)—corporate and national
- the derivatives market (basically bets in various markets) is estimated to be worth ten × global GDP—that is $100,000,000,000,000,000 (a quadrillion dollars)

It's just too big to comprehend. To put it in perspective, if you stacked dollar bills one on top of the other, the tower of money would stretch from Earth to Venus three times.

A huge amount of this money is in investment funds, family wealth funds, insurance companies, pension funds, etc. It is in hot, sandy countries with low tax costs. It creates quite a bit of employment for the finance industry but doesn't help society in any meaningful way. The money in the world is disconnected from the value in the world. Why does a pension fund or a venture capitalist choose to invest in "bets" rather than in all the value that is created by hardworking entrepreneurs?

Some money finds its way into the start-up world, but start-ups are over-glamorized; they are the roulette-wheel of entrepreneurship and 80% or more fail. And when they do, the streets are littered with their victims; people lose their livelihoods, their homes, and their families' and friends' money. It gets messy. But start-ups still get all the attention.

Companies that have survived start-up are a much better bet: they have a great product, great customers, and real revenues and profits. They have created a brand that people like and trust, so they generate sales and profits. These are the people we need more of. These are the people we need to help. These are the people we need to go and do deals with.

There are three key reasons the big money doesn't follow the value of investing in SMEs:

1. Risk—small companies are too risky. They lose a couple of key clients or key staff and have their worst year ever (or maybe their last).
2. Scale—I call this the scale paradox: you have to be big to get big. If you are not already a big company, it is hard to win the huge global contracts, and you can't get big unless you win the big global contracts.

3. Liquidity—small companies are illiquid. If you invest, it takes ages to get your money back. Three- to five-year-year plans can easily slip into ten- to fifteen-year plans, and global capital likes to be able to rotate between asset classes as the economic winds change.

You can address the disconnect between value and capital though agglomeration (virtual merger 2.0) by clustering the best SMEs and publicly listing them, lowering the risk, and creating scale and liquidity.

The impact of this is twofold.

First, for entrepreneurs, it creates a connection between global capital and the value they have created. And, as a side effect, it makes them wealthy. This wealth, I believe, creates a meritocracy. It sends a message to the next generation that, if you take some risks, and you can build a great business, add value to society and employ people. You can become wealthy. This will encourage others to follow in the same footsteps. Also, first-generation wealthy people are generous: they spend their money and are philanthropic. Give money to entrepreneurs and they go on to solve bigger problems, or they spend it in their communities and create a real trickle-down effect.

Second, we are not all entrepreneurs, but we can unlock the trapped value in the SME space for ordinary investors. The financial markets have become a slaughterhouse for investors in recent history, where one seems to play a zero-sum game with the greediest people on the planet. Investing in bonds or equities is often described as "risk on" or "risk off" investing, but with the bubbles in both the share and bond markets, it is "risk on" or "more risk on" right now. I genuinely believe that through agglomeration, we can also make investments for ordinary investors that are profitable, debt-free, fast growing, well-diversified, and pay a dividend by accessing a previously completely untapped part of the economy that also happens to be by far and away its biggest part.

Agglomeration has the power to redistribute trillions of dollars throughout the world but, instead of creating state dependency, it is distributing it in a meritocratic way to the people in society who work hard, take risks, solve problems, and create jobs. The rewards and upside go to the ordinary people who back them by buying the shares.

When you have a company, why not look for others in the same sector? One of the biggest drivers of value is scale. Big companies are much more valuable than small ones, and a big one can just as easily be several small ones put together, so when you have a company, can you roll up? You can read my book, Agglomerate: From Idea to IPO in 12 Months, for my take on doing huge roll-ups without cash or debt. It also tackles many of the issues on integration, culture, and value retention. This is about how to put deals together with hundreds of millions of value but with normal, small, profitable, debt-free companies, good businesses, not distressed but sub-scale from a capital markets perspective.

The world is a little bit unfair when it comes to SME owners. Effectively, if you're running an SME, it's difficult to access capital, to grow beyond a certain size, and to get banks to support you with simple things like international credit card payments or the basic things you need to be able to grow your business. With my experience, having done dozens of different deals, I wanted to fix this problem.

Scale, Liquidity and, Risk

The idea behind virtual merger 2.0 or "agglomeration," as we call it, is a way to tackle those three issues—risk, scale, and liquidity—and therefore create huge amounts of shareholder value. In the private equity world, they "roll up," which means they put a number of companies in the same industry together, and you then have the sum total of all of the parts. You shove them all into one box and off you go.

The challenge with owner-managed SMEs is that they're below the private equity radar. These are companies that are generating profits of between $500,000 and $5 million a year. They are often lifestyle businesses that have been going for 10+ years and are generating seven-figure profits for the owners but, basically, they're not hitting it out of the park. They've pretty much plateaued in terms of their growth. They've reached their glass ceiling, and it's hard for them to break through. They're great businesses, but they can't really go much further from where they are. Often, these people are ambitious, they want to buy their competitors, they want to expand overseas, they want to do things, but they can't, and they feel a bit trapped. They feel like they're swinging their arms and not landing that many punches.

We look for these companies. Now, the challenge with these companies is they're run by maverick owners who are very successful. You often find that they have written books about their particular business niche. They might appear on TV occasionally, commenting on their industry. They are key people in their particular industry, and they don't integrate well. So, if you use a traditional roll-up method, the unique brand and culture that they've created with their staff and with their customers won't really mix. You can't shove it all into one box and expect it to be the same.

So, by doing the traditional roll-up, you end up destroying value instead of creating value. You think you're being clever by executing all these synergies and getting rid of bookkeepers, but all you're really doing is annoying the key talent and the key customers of the company by trying to change everything. Everybody hates change, so by trying to change everything, you're trying to fill a bathtub with a sieve; you think you're making progress, but when you look in the bath, there's not much there. So, my experience of roll-ups in that SME owner-managed space is that they don't really work effectively and, particularly, the synergies are fool's gold: you can never really extract the value that you want to.

I decided to approach this in a completely different way by creating a common holding company—a publicly listed holding company—that is shared by a number of business owners in the same sector. In effect, they swap their shares in their private company for shares in the public company and, collectively, they own the majority of that publicly listed company. Now, each person is still responsible for running their own business, but they can't tell each other how to run each other's business—they're all equal. They form what's called a "founders board," so they can effectively make collective decisions on how they cooperate together, but they're not actually able to tell each other what to do.

These businesses effectively co-own the listed company, so what you end up with is a listed company that can report its accounts as the sum total of all the subsidiaries. If you have ten subsidiaries and they're each doing $1 million of profit, you've now got a listed company that's making $10 million profit a year, and there's a huge difference between the valuation of a public company doing $10 million a year in profit versus a private company doing $1 million a year in profit.

Business Breakout: The Liquidity Discount

Looking at the value of a large public company versus its private peer, you'll often find there's a discount of about 30% between those two companies because the public company is more liquid, and you can buy and sell their shares on the stock market. To do a sale of a large private company could take nine to eighteen months, with all the due diligence necessary. The decision to sell has a really long-term horizon until the actual liquidity event, and there's plenty that can go wrong in the meantime. Liquidity is a huge issue for investors. They want the ability to rotate their capital between different types of investment according to which way the economic winds are blowing.

> The discount between a large public company and a small private company can be a ten times difference in valuation. The small company will sell for three-or four-times earnings, and the large public company will sell for thirty- or forty-times earnings, so a huge arbitrage can be gained by people joining the agglomeration structure.

The three key issues of risk, scale, and liquidity are all addressed through the common holding company structure:

1. You're a lower risk because you're a portfolio of independent limited companies so, if one of them fails, it doesn't affect the whole. They're diversified across different products, services, countries and currencies, thereby creating a lower risk profile.
2. You have the scale with the big public company you can point to, so now you can win bigger contracts, apply for government contracts or bids for large businesses and benefit from the credibility that comes from being a fully reporting public company.
3. You have the liquidity because you're now a public company, so you get that liquidity push-up in valuation, effectively, all the components of the deal get a much larger valuation.

The person who puts the deal together ends up with a slice of the company at the top, so it's easy for you to wind up with a decent share of the whole thing. It's fairly easy to put the deal together on a no-money-down basis. We already have publicly-listed companies in various sectors so, if you bring us deals, we can take them public for you very quickly. But you can also do this yourself.

You can create a holding company and take it public. When you list a public company, depending on which exchange you list on, you have to have a free float, so you have to have a percentage of shares that are owned by independent, third-party members of the public. That free float is a way to raise a bit of money and use that money to pay for the listing. So, effectively, it can be a completely self-financing structure, and it can be big.

At the Harbour Club, we go through a warts-and-all case study because we've made quite a lot of mistakes. In effect, we created $300 million of market capitalization in the holding company's first ninety days using this structure. My personal stake in this holding company was worth €50 million at one point. It's a powerful structure for growing quickly and adding lots of shareholder value.

This structure is a real game-changer. It potentially unlocks the value that's being left on the table. The small business sector represents 50% of the economy in most mature markets, trillions of dollars of value across the globe. It's a surprisingly easy conversation to have with business owners because you're helping them to go public, they retain their independence, they can continue to run the business in the same way, but they create an enormous amount of shareholder value for them and their families.

A lot of the no-money-down strategies I talk about at the Harbour Club are dealing with distressed and motivated sellers. For an agglomeration, you're talking to people who are solvent, they're debt-free, they're doing well, but they just feel like they could do better. They want to fulfill their ambitions, that dream they had when they came up with the idea for this company. This is an opportunity for them to effectively create something truly game-changing and different within their particular sector.

Deal Deep Dive: Scale, Liquidity, and Reduced Risks

Goran did the Harbour Club course in March 2015 in Mallorca. He was intrigued by mergers and acquisitions and inspired by the idea of doing global deals, but he had no experience. He decided to learn to do deals by actually doing them, after learning as much as he could from the course.

The agglomeration model and the idea of fragmented markets got him thinking, so he had a look through his telephone contacts to see which companies he knew. He chose the telecom and cable TV industry, which has over 6,000 businesses in Europe. He knew one entrepreneur in that field. From his research, he identified more than eighty businesses were too small to scale, and their business value was dropping because they were losing users, therefore decreasing the exit value of the business. The telco and cable TV industry is a dynamic M&A industry with the bigger telco and cable TV companies frequently acquiring smaller companies.

Goran realized that he would need to get to know the industry in-depth to close deals. He determined the size of the fragmented market and analyzed all possible competitors.

He did his research. He had more than 200 live meetings and video calls with telco and cable owners to find out where their problems were. He wanted to identify the pain points in the industry and check with the business owners in the segment to identify what they would need to succeed. It was also really important to understand the mindset of the owners, how they were thinking, what their personal motivations were, what they wanted for themselves.

Among the bottom-line pain points were that the owners wanted to remain independent as entrepreneurs; they needed cost savings, and they found the price of content rights high. They also had challenges investing in technology and infrastructure. Adding new services was important and, perhaps most of all, the owners didn't want to sell their business. If they could solve these problems, they would have an advantage and could compete with the big players in the market. It is important to remember that the companies required in an agglomeration are profitable, so it's imperative that the deal will solve their three main problems—risk, scale, and liquidity—which are also problems for the whole industry.

The agglomeration model is perfect for solving all these problems, reducing risk, and creating shareholder value. The agglomeration will bring the smaller companies together, so they collaborate with one another and enjoy the benefits of scale, liquidity, and reduced risks. As a group, they are stronger and can avoid being the target of a takeover.

Goran set up two types of deal structures:

1. Swapping shares with the listed company
2. Becoming a client for the content of the listed company, thereby giving the group more buying power

Pitching to businesses works better if you have people from the industry on your team because they give credibility. You need to adjust the pitch in order for business owners to really understand it, and many business owners need multiple talks and negotiations to get on board with the idea. It's not just about explaining the plan, but more about building a vision for the business owner. Rapport is vital. Goran realized that the biggest challenge for business owners was changing their mindset. They needed to stop thinking like managers and change to shareholder thinking, in other words, from operational tasks to strategic thinking.

For Goran, it was important that he was able to close deals as fast as possible by immediately collecting accounts, preparing offers, doing due diligence, signing agreements, doing the legal documentation, etc. This was also a great way to identify which companies were serious about the idea and which were curious timewasters. There was no time to waste. Being prepared was crucial, along with having a pipeline of other interested companies, so momentum continued when one dropped out.

Goran notes, "In the beginning, you will lose a lot of your time, so get used to it. Everybody is lying and saying they are the best. It takes persistence, so don't lose your faith and vision of what you want to do."

From the other side of the deal, Goran got as many investors lined up with as much money as possible, so that they could invest in the pre-IPO stage, and for support doing the deals as the agglomeration started.

The final agglomeration involved deals with companies in eight different countries. Therefore, he needed to find local legal companies that understood deals and acquisitions from the local perspective. He also needed his own legal agreements and team.

Goran said, "I came into this with zero experience doing M&A deals, and from the start, everything went wrong—positioning myself, the pitch, making offers, getting clear on the process. We didn't have a good number of investors at the start. If we did, we could have moved faster."

Goran is currently in the end phase of the deal before listing the agglomerated company on a stock market. He is dealing with a pipeline of sixty companies in the telco and cable segment in eight different countries in Eastern Europe. So far, it has been a steep learning experience, but he's looking forward to capitalizing on the deals that are lined up.

Part Four

What To Do After You've Done The Deal

Doing a deal is about empathy. Before you judge a person, you must walk a mile in their shoes—that way you are a mile away...and you have their shoes.

A Note on Selling and on Exiting

And now what? It is really tempting to keep the business you've bought. Business is such an emotional thing, and as an entrepreneur, you have to develop a keen emotional maturity about it. It is easy to keep everything and to love them like your children. Trust me, they don't love you back (the businesses I mean, of course, your children love you!).

When asked when the right time is to sell a good business, Warren Buffett says, "Never..." Well, these are not good businesses, and the only thing worse than a bad business is ten bad businesses. These are small businesses, which may be good in their tiny niche, but are fragile, delicate, and require constant attention. When you have one, you should build shareholder value, and you should sell. Create a capital event, learn something valuable, and move on to the next one.

CHAPTER 14

ADDING SHAREHOLDER
VALUE AND THE EXIT

Cash is king!

Your best customer is the person who buys your business. It's true. When you think about being customer-focused, you have to consider the things you can do that will either increase the value of the business (i.e., adding shareholder value) or decrease the time it will take to sell the business (your exit).

Now, as entrepreneurs, we love to solve problems, and those problems usually revolve around staff and customers. We want to create a team and a culture that is high performance as well as fun and exciting. We want to create products and services that disrupt and amaze. The happy side effect of having a great company culture, excellent teamwork, and exceptional products is value creation.

I want to try turning that belief upside down and focus on the value creation first: identifying the drivers of shareholder value and then doing those things. Quite often, they can be counter-intuitive—like selling less, for example—but more on that in a moment.

When you embark on a traditional business turnaround program—let's call it a "value-creation" program (because the business might not need to be turned around, but all businesses could benefit from the creation of more value)—many of the things you'd probably think to do might not actually realize any more value in the short- to medium-term. For example, with new sales and marketing campaigns, the cost of acquiring a new customer is sometimes far greater than the money you make from that customer in the first twelve months. So sometimes, counterintuitively, it's actually better to stop doing expensive sales and marketing campaigns and focus on your current customers. Focus on profitability because that's really going to drive the overall value of the business.

Cash is King!

So, how do you create shareholder value when you first take over a company? The first area to focus on would be cash, because cash is king. Businesses don't fail from a lack of profit—they fail from a lack of cash, so having a keen focus on cash and cash generation is a number one priority:

- Stop all expenditures that don't help your cash flow and focus on collecting money in a timely fashion
- Don't provide credit terms to risky customers
- Prioritize payments on a business-critical basis

Too many businesses get stuck in the "squeaky wheel gets the grease" syndrome, whereby they're paying the people who call and complain the most. You may find businesses that haven't paid their staff, but they've paid less important suppliers. Get the right focus.

You can do this by making a list of all the people you owe money to and then breaking it down into the order that you're going to pay them. Effectively no one in the middle third of the list gets paid until all the creditors in the top third are paid, and no one in bottom third gets paid until all those in the middle third are paid. This is a really good business discipline. It sounds ridiculously simple, and implementing this system can help cash management enormously.

It's also really worth doing a daily or weekly cash flow for the business. Keep it simple, a money in/money out spreadsheet with a running bank balance along the bottom. By laying things out in a simple form directly in front of you and seeing what impact it has on your bank balance, you can get plenty of ideas and clues as to how to make your cash flow work better. Perhaps you could settle half an invoice now and half in a couple of weeks? It might annoy the person at the suppliers a little bit, but at least, if you've made an offer to pay them in full and it's in a relatively short space of time, they're probably not going to take any legal action against you.

Pick the Low-Hanging Fruit

Every business has low-hanging fruit. Could you increase the prices? In most businesses that I've come across, the pricing policies seem to be related to the age of the owner. The older the owner is, the less often they've raised their prices, or they still haven't properly factored in inflation. In most companies, any increase in pricing goes straight to the bottom line because it's 100% additional profit. For an average company, a 5% increase in prices is a 40% increase in profit, and a 40% increase in profit is multiplied up when you sell the company. This has a huge impact on shareholder value. There have been many studies of customer attrition and price increases, and it's generally accepted that a single-digit percentage increase every three years has little effect on customer attrition, and any effect that it does have is mitigated by the additional profit that's generated.

Are there things that can be outsourced? In many small businesses, most of the tasks and functions within the business are an odd size. In a large company, it's easy to have a finance department or a marketing department, whereas in a small company, you might need 75% of a finance person, 50% of a bookkeeper, and 25% of a marketing person. In these situations, sometimes using an outsourced provider can be a more efficient way of handling some of the functions within the business.

Get rid of all the little expenses that accumulate over the years. For example: software licenses, the bubbling water cooler in the corner, the stamp machine (even though you don't send out letters anymore), expensive photocopying contracts (even though you only use the machine as a scanner). These things mount up and accumulate within businesses but can be easily be done away with.

When you look at all these expenses, you have to mentally multiply them up for the impact that they're having on the overall sale price of the business. You need a keen eye on all the different things that are going on in the business and where the money is being spent.

There is a story that when Philip Green (a British billionaire businessman) first bought BHS (a once large retail chain in the UK), the first thing he did was save $1 million a week on coat hangers.

Once you've gone through the figures and done the cash flow and profit management tasks, the next thing is to get the business ready for sale.

The Virtual Data Room

A virtual data room is a fancy-sounding name for a repository of all the company's key documents, which people doing due diligence can access. Having an up-to-date data room will shave months off a transaction, so it is worth putting in place and getting right at the beginning.

What goes in there? Well, if you google "due diligence questionnaire," you'll find loads of different online resources about the things that you need to have in a due diligence pack. While "the virtual data room" sounds glamorous, it is just an online document storage system that holds all the data needed.

You can use Google Docs, Dropbox, or any type of cloud storage provider. Each of the questions in the due diligence questionnaires becomes a folder stored online, containing, for example, the company's:

- accounts
- bank statements
- contracts with suppliers
- contracts with customers
- contracts with employees
- insurance documents
- leases
- loan agreements
- anything else relevant to the business

You might find that there are several questions on the due diligence questionnaires that aren't relevant to your business because these questionnaires are designed to cover everything from a power station to a corner shop. My advice in this situation is always to put something in the folder. Perhaps it asks for a copy of your professional indemnity insurance certificate, but you're a small retailer, and, clearly, you're not offering any professional advice, and therefore, you don't need professional indemnity insurance. Simply include a letter signed by the directors of the company, explaining that you don't have professional indemnity insurance because you don't provide professional advice, and therefore, it's not needed.

Due diligence can drag on for a long time if your information isn't readily available. Make sure you address each question to eliminate any potential questions an acquirer could ask that could delay the acquisition process. Anything you can do to create a path of least resistance when it comes to due diligence is very important.

This is what brokers should be telling you to do, but most brokers don't. The first time you have an inquiry about the business, it seems like there's an incredible amount of work to be done, with hundreds of painful questions, but buyers need this information to make a decision, particularly if they have external investors, a lender, or a bank involved in the transaction.

If you have all this information ready and waiting, you will be head and shoulders above the competition. You will look organized and efficient. And as they say, "How you do anything is how you do everything." Get the information ready upfront so there are no surprises. Maintain your virtual data room, so that when you've got an inquiry, you're ready to sell.

Now you're ready to start the sales process and look for potential buyers.

Time to Sell

When you're looking for deals to acquire a company, you'll find not many people want to help you, particularly when you're looking for distressed deals. There might be a bit of professional jealousy; after all, as I mentioned earlier, nobody wants to give you the dusty painting they found in the attic and then find out it was a Picasso. There's frequently resistance when people don't want to help you in the sourcing side of doing deals. However, when it comes to selling a business, there's social capital associated with knowing people who sell businesses. People like to share; they like to help you find opportunities. When it comes to selling, you'll find a lot of people share information around. Knowing people who are selling businesses makes them look good. Start telling everyone you've ever met, email people, and put it on social media that you have this business for sale.

Initially, people will inquire about the business, so send them an executive summary, a one-page description of the business, and some highlights. If they're interested at that point, you might ask them to enter into a non-disclosure agreement and then give them a full information memorandum. The next step is providing an indicative term sheet and giving them access to the due diligence folders. It's just like a normal sales and marketing process, but with quite a few extra moving parts.

 Deal Deep Dive: Business Improvement

Back in 2009, in a joint venture deal with four Harbour Club delegates, we bought an air-conditioning company. It was twenty-three years old and had blue-chip retail and local government clients but had gotten itself into a bit of a financial pickle. It was the peak of the global financial crises, and its revenue had plummeted. What was left had fairly solid maintenance revenue, but the company had been paying random suppliers (who were presumably the loudest ones), not paying staff or other important bills, and had reached the of the line. We acquired the whole company for $1 and immediately started to manage the business on a cash basis. Within six weeks, we had caught up on two months of unpaid salaries and started to get on top of the other creditors. We then wanted to prepare the business for sale, so we went in as a team to assess what we could prepare for sale. The Harbour Club delegates were all experts in their fields, with great commercial and entrepreneurial experience. They drafted a forty-point plan on improvement measures that could be done across the whole business. It was quite an impressive report but, to demonstrate the shift between customer value and shareholder value, I invited the CEO of what was at the time the world's largest business brokerage to go through the report with one critical focus: "Which of these things will improve the price or allow us to sell faster?" The answer was none of it.

What the broker did say was that this report was an excellent sales tool, so when selling the company, you could say, "Here are the forty things we have identified that you could do to massively improve the business." Can you see how easy it might be to get lost in the weeds of actually trying to do all that, getting yourself busy while you are wasting valuable time, spending profits, and not actually adding any value? It's a lesson I had to learn more than once. (Don't you hate learning lessons more than once? So frustrating!) Entrepreneurs have the overwhelming self-belief that they can make wonderful things happen. I guess that if we didn't think like that, we wouldn't be entrepreneurs. But if it is not creating value and it is just taking up time, why do it?

The next great lesson from that same deal happened when it came to selling. We had the perfect buyer after just four months. He had gone through due diligence, had cash in the bank, and everything was rosy. Suddenly his accountant told him that this business would not qualify for a hoped-for tax relief, and the deal fell through. It took another seven months to sell the business. The lesson there was to always keep two horses in the race—just because you have a buyer, don't stop looking for other buyers!

———————

CHAPTER 15

SHOULD YOU STAY OR SHOULD YOU GO?

When is the right time to sell your business? Now.

If you're wondering what to do after you've gotten into the deal, then my advice is you sell. Pretty much every reason you can think of for not selling your business is probably a reason for selling your business.

Many moons ago, I owned two companies at the same time. One was a call center business that was incredibly profitable. We had a three-year contract with the world's largest insurance company, AIG, and we were making over $200,000 per quarter in net cash. It was a really great business. I had another business in the telecom space, which was doing okay, but wasn't really increasing shareholder value year after year. My conventional thinking at the time was to sell the telecom company, which was limping along, and to keep the cash cow call center that was generating all the cash.

I went through the sales process on the telecom company, which took a while, and by the time I had sold it, the call center company had failed due to issues with AIG. We had many problems with them, as I'm sure many other companies did as well.

My reason *for not selling* was that I had a three-year contract with the world's largest insurance company.

My reason *for selling* should have been because I had a three-year contract with the world's largest insurance company.

If you're a business owner and you're thinking that next year is going to be your best year ever, then sell it now. If next year is going to be your best year ever, the buyer is going to love your business. De-risk the deal, sell the business at what it's worth today with an earn-out linked to its performance next year. So, when it doesn't actually do what you expected to do because, "Hey, this is business, and when has it ever done exactly what you expected it to do?" You get the upside if it succeeds, and you don't have the risk of the downside if it fails.

Don't Obsess!

People get obsessed with the business that they're in. They think it's the last business they're ever going to have. They want to sell it for $50 million, and if they can't get $50 million, they don't want to sell their baby.

This is my perspective. For the first twenty years of your life, you're pretty much useless. You're still learning how everything works. The last twenty years of your life, you're also probably pretty useless. You've got this kind of sweet spot in the middle where you have enough energy to get things done, and, from an emotional and intellectual perspective, you're firing on all four cylinders. If you're really lucky, you get eighty years of life. That bit in the middle is only forty years. So, if you think about running a business for ten or twenty years, you're talking about devoting 25% to 50%, of your useful time on the planet to this one business idea.

For me, that's quite a frightening prospect. As entrepreneurs, we're full of ideas. We have lots of things that we want to do, and we have things that we want to change about the world around us.

Are you really going to spend half your useful life running one business? You make money when you sell. I always used to think running a business was about income—that as long as you have a really high income, you can have a high standard of living. The passive income myth perpetuates this idea that you set up these little businesses and it's all wonderful. But businesses are constantly evolving; the landscape is changing. The way you acquire customers is changing all the time. Marketing that worked last week doesn't work next week; you have staff, you have customers, you have stress. You really can't create *passive* income from a business.

Business Breakout: Passive Income Property Myth

Everybody thinks properties are passive investments. They are not. You have changing interest rates, broken furnaces, bad tenants, downtime, and defaults; there are all sorts of things to consider and manage. You're not really a property investor: you have a property business. It has customers, the tenants. There are operational aspects, such as the management of the property. You can outsource the management, but then you end up with a lower rate of return, probably lower than just buying a government bond.

The only real passive income comes from capital. Capital deployed generates genuinely passive types of income come rain or shine.

Multiple Mini-Capital Events

Your main goal should be to create capital. Rather than having one big goal of a capital event right at the end of your career, try and have multiple mini- capital events throughout your career.

You don't make money running businesses. You make money when you sell them. You need to create these capital events often.

Entrepreneurs aren't particularly well-prepared for selling businesses. It probably took you years to hone the skill of how you sell your products to customers. The same thing is true when it comes to selling a company. I know you have a three- to five-year plan to sell your business, but trust me, it won't be three to five years. It never is. So, if you wait fifty years, until the end of your business life, and then try to sell your company, you will have zero experience of selling a company. The first time you sell a company, you'll learn loads of lessons about how difficult it is to find the buyer and get the deal closed. Invariably, people aren't successful the first time they do something.

So rather than having all of your eggs in a basket that's extremely high-risk because you don't have the skillset, why not hone your skillset? Why not learn how to sell businesses?

On the flip side, if you are going to do a start-up every time, you basically waste three years while you're coming up with names, creating logos, and trying to get your first customer. You are pushing a massive rock up a hill. Then you have a period when you can actually build the business and make some money. Then you could sell it. If you're really good at selling, you're probably into a five- to ten-year cycle to sell a business.

If you buy a business that's already pushed the rock up the hill and now the rock is just gently rolling down the other side, you can do a lot more of these deals. In fact, you can do several a year by buying a business that is already established, making it look much better, and then selling it again.

The Great Thing About Capital Events Versus Income

Income is just what you spend. In fact, if you are like most ambitious people, income is probably about 20% less than you spend. Oscar Wilde said that somebody who lived within their means lacked imagination: your lifestyle always adjusts to your income, and you don't really make any steps forward from a wealth perspective. But when you have a capital event, you can use the capital to generate passive income through investment. You can then start to live on the income from your investment. That means you can now invest all your income.

This is quite different from the advice of most of the books and wealth advisers out there. Most advice is designed around typical employees and having multiple pots. You have one pot for a rainy day, one pot for emergencies, another that you never touch, and a pot that you can touch—all this kind of nonsense. They advise you to save 10% or 15% or 20% of your income, and if you do that, you know you'll have a million dollars saved by the time you're 192 years old. I don't buy that as being a credible way to get any wealth.

Your goal? What percentage of your income should you be saving? You should be saving 100% of your income. The only way you can save 100% of your income is if you're able to live off the income from your investments.

So, by creating these capital events, you can then deploy this capital into passive investments—real passive investments, not the ones you see advertised on the internet—and use this passive income to live on.

Tim Ferriss, in *The 4-Hour Work Week*, talked about mini-retirements and taking three to four-month sabbaticals, where you re-energize, re-engage, do something completely different, and then come back and smash your business for a few months. I look at it more from a capital and finance perspective, which is about mini-capital events. You can build the wealth that gives you the comfort and control over your own finances and puts you in a powerful position.

So, the right time to sell the business is now, because you'll create that capital event that takes all the pressure off. After that, your decision-making process, and everything else you do, is much better. It's a way for you to grow personally.

 ### Deal Deep Dive: The World of Private Wealth Banking

I often hear people giving wealth advice, whether it's in books or on websites or YouTube videos, telling you to save 15% of your income or whatever their magic number is. I think that if these people were actually genuinely wealthy, they would know what happens when you become wealthy. When you become wealthy, you have access to private wealth banking, and private wealth banking is the conspiracy come true.

When I was younger, I always heard, "Everything is designed so the rich get richer, and the poor stay poor." I used to think that was just cynicism and people trying to disparage the other side—the politics of envy. Then, when I became wealthy, I gained access to private wealth banking, and I realized it was true. You really do have an unfair advantage when you already have money. Private wealth banking—I'm talking about banks like UBS, Morgan Stanley, and Credit Suisse to name a few.

This is not to be mistaken with private banking. Private banking is where you get a fancy credit card and a person who answers the phone quickly—nothing to do with private wealth.

In private wealth banking, there are no cards, no checkbooks. You get access to products that people who are not wealthy are not allowed to access. You have access to investment products that:

- you can manage in a way that protects you from big market swings

- provide much higher returns, higher rates of income, and lower management fees

Within private wealth banking, you get Lombard (collateralized) lending, enabling you to use that core portfolio effectively as an asset to borrow money against. For example, if you had $100,000 and you bought a $100,000 bond with your bank, you might be able to get leverage on that bond, so they might lend you 50% or 70% of the value of the bond for maybe 3% above the bank's interest rate. The bank will normally insist that the leverage is then reinvested with the bank and used to buy more bonds or more stocks. This often unravels horribly in times of economic crisis, when there's an adjustment in the value of the underlying assets and everybody takes a huge bath (i.e., loses money).

Lombard lending is open to private wealth clients, and you can borrow huge amounts of money at low interest rates without conditions on its use. At the time of writing, my bank will lend you euros at 0.7% a year, secured against your portfolio.

Put that into context: if you bought a Bentley for $100,000 and you bought it using the Lombard loan, it would cost you $700 a year. When you sell the asset, you have the depreciation (or appreciation) cost over the time that you've owned it, but basically the cost of capital for that period of time would be $700 a year. Would you like a Bentley for $700 a year, plus the depreciation? I don't think you have to be asked twice. Of course, you don't have to buy depreciating assets. You can make any investment you choose: property, art, bonds, stocks, or whatever.

You can use Lombard lending to buy more assets. For example, you can buy other assets that provide income. You can have your core portfolio, which is providing income, and then buy a real estate investment trust (REIT), which is effectively publicly listed property.

It's property, but it's liquid, so you can buy it in the morning and sell it in the afternoon. That gives you exposure to property, a nice, regular income that comes in from the rental payments, and the exposure to capital appreciation on the property. REITs often have double-digit annual returns, and some of them pay monthly or quarterly.

The tricky thing with the traditional savings plans when you're looking at saving 15% of your income is that you save 15% of your income and then that's it. You can't lay your hands on it. With private wealth banking, you can save 100% of your income and, if you do need some cash for a deal or a transaction, you can simply draw cash out immediately. It's like you've tied up your money in investments, but you've still got access to cash. It's a very flexible way of dealing with money and a great way of managing capital purchases such as planes, boats, and cars.

Most of the banks need you to have $10 million of investable assets to let you on the private wealth-banking ladder. Some will consider a starting point a little bit lower, maybe $3 million, if they can see that there's an opportunity to work with you to get up to that $10 million over a reasonable period.

So, your first goal is to get on the private wealth-banking ladder, because it's an absolute game-changer in terms of your wealth. Forget what the seminar speakers say about wealth. They probably didn't make the grade, and so are only talking about their understanding of wealth management based on their own financial circumstances. Also, people whom you think are wealthy are often just asset rich, but totally illiquid. If you look at real wealth—the family offices, the family trusts, etc.— they all use this kind of banking relationship. At the Harbour Club, I quite often show examples of private wealth product offerings, and you would be staggered by what is on offer.

———————

CONCLUSION

O ur only options are to be informed, uninformed, or misinformed. I hope you feel inspired to climb onto the next rung of the entrepreneurial ladder, to "go do deals," and that I may have challenged some conventional wisdom about how it is really done.

It isn't easy—nothing worth having is—but I believe it is a better, more efficient, and more exciting way to use your entrepreneurial skills. It's an area of business worth learning about and understanding better for your own wealth and that of the world.

I am passionate about empowering entrepreneurs and helping to democratize wealth in a meritocratic way, and I hope you will join me in that quest.

Remember, you can't help the poor by being one of them. When you are truly free, you can help others to join you on the same path.

What Next?

I have saved the best ideas for the Harbour Club itself, to be fair to the people who choose to invest in their own development, but I've shared plenty of tactics throughout the book to whet your appetite.

Here are some of the extra tactics and strategies taught on the course:

- **The deal team is just a big interference:** Learn why it is completely wrong thinking to surround yourself with advisers to do a deal. It can seem like a crutch to support a lack of confidence, but it ruins deals and means you have expenses, whether you transact or not. Smart dealmakers know how to make deals, self-finance, and when to use external advisers.

- **Personal guarantee magic:** Find out how to make "personal guarantees" disappear using this financial engineering strategy (it works on most SME businesses).

- **Qualifying leads:** Discover why $500,000–$5 million revenue companies are in the sweet spot for doing deals.

- **Three research tools:** How to find an endless supply of leads and how to pick the right industry.

- **Eleven psychological triggers of a motivated seller:** Understanding these triggers is the key to unlocking the creative deal structures that give sellers what they want while structuring a deal for no money up front without borrowing or debt. Once you understand these triggers, then creating a win-win deal will be effortless.

- **The perfect storm:** When three of these triggers are combined, you are much more likely to close the deal.

- **"I hate due diligence":** It's expensive, boring, and time-consuming, but necessary, right? What if you could get your due diligence done for free without any extra work, and even better, have it more complete than if you did it yourself or paid

$100,000 to hire professionals to do the job for you? Find out how on Day Two of the course.

- **Insolvency secrets:** Discover how to buy companies through the insolvency process using these five proven deal templates (100% legal).

- **Easy cash injection:** Discover how to take a company with ten or more employees and inject up to 15% of their yearly revenue back into the business as cash. It only takes one phone call to do and requires no upfront cash.

- **Bulletproof purchase agreement:** How to turn the simple, age-old purchase agreement into a contract more powerful than anything a lawyer could ever draft (no legal experience required). This is out-of-the-box thinking, but it's so powerful that a bankruptcy attorney working for one of the largest accountancy firms in the UK now recommends this strategy to all his clients.

- **Compete clause:** How to stop the previous business owners from stealing your best staff and customers and going into direct competition with you. Non-competes are no longer viable in some places; they are a violation of human rights under EU law. Discover one simple strategy and get your hands on a proven contract template you can use that will leave you secretly wishing they do steal your customers.

- **Financial engineering:** Find out about amazing tactics to uncover profit hidden in your business without increasing sales. If your business' gross annual revenue is $500,000 or more, then this alone could recoup your course fee within a couple of weeks of returning home.

- **Cash is king:** Discover the three-step formula for fixing the long-term cash-flow problems in almost any type of business.

You don't go broke from a lack of sales, profit, or gross annual revenue: it's a lack of cash that will bury you alive.

Find out more at https://harbourclubusa.com/.

ACKNOWLEDGMENTS

I want to thank the team at Unity, past and present, for their support through the peaks of ecstasy to the depths of despair. We win together and we lose together, but as long as we win more than we lose, we progress, and we learn.

Also, thanks to my Harbour Club inner circle for the constant encouragement and for the great examples of deals that happen around us all the time, taking our learning forward, and giving great inspiration to the new people coming through.

Finally, to the Harbour Club team: they have made my ramblings into a truly unique and amazing product. I would never have created it without you—I would have been too busy doing deals.

THE AUTHOR

Jeremy lives in Singapore with his wife and two children. He also has homes in Mallorca, Spain, and Ukraine. He is actively involved in buying and selling SMEs around the world and has business interests in twelve countries at the time of writing.

During a career spanning over twenty years, Jeremy has started many businesses and has grown his organization to employing more than 130 people, with over £10m in revenue. In recent years, he has completed well over fifty transactions, with both distressed and solvent businesses and advised on hundreds more.

He also has an in-depth knowledge of insolvency and company law, and a gift for devising creative deal structures that require little or no funding and no bank leverage. Renowned for being truly agnostic in his business interests, his track record includes a health club and spa, music school, IT support, telecoms, training, business process outsourcing, cleaning, air conditioning, and a cooking school, just to name a few.

More recently, Jeremy has focused on bigger deals involving capital markets, reverse mergers, and public listings, and he even bought a bank.

He has also been teaching mergers and acquisitions (M&A) tactics through his Harbour Club program since 2009, specializing in deals that do not require cash up front. Jeremy loves education but hates the cheesy seminar that has all the razzmatazz but is skinny on content. The Harbour Club is the opposite—there is possibly even too much content!

Go to www.harbourclubevents.com for the stories of past delegates or to sign up for the newsletter.

Printed in the USA
CPSIA information can be obtained
at www.ICGtesting.com
JSHW021956150824
68134JS00055B/1752

9 781631 952937